Curt,

Thank you for your leadership. Your service. Your friendship. Stay

KEVIN A. RICE
LEADERSHIP FOREWARNED

*Preventing Bad Things From Happening
to Good Organizations*

Print ISBN: 978-1-09831-654-9

eBook ISBN: 978-1-09831-654-9

TABLE OF CONTENTS

ACKNOWLEDGMENTS

To Cynthia, my beautiful wife of twenty-five years, as I always say, I married above myself. Thanks to Phil Carlson for his friendship and his contributions in a hundred different ways. To the boys in that band, those four Secret Service agents that are more like brothers to me than friends. I was never really the leader of that band, but I appreciated that moniker more than you will ever know.

To my Mom and Dad, words cannot express my love and appreciation.

Thanks to Maryann and Janet, two rock stars in the HR field, for their insight and their support.

Lastly, and this might sound crass, but I want to acknowledge the HR and business leaders I have witnessed act in hundreds of unsafe and unwise ways. If it wasn't for you, I would have never put pen to paper. Your actions in the past may make for safer work environments in the future.

- Kevin Rice

FOREWORD

There is a great quote attributed to boxer Mike Tyson which says, "Everyone has a plan until they get punched in the mouth." It sounds good, but is it really true? As a professional involved in law enforcement for over thirty years, at all levels of government, I have been well-trained on situational awareness, as well as identifying and mitigating risks. My training also includes the use the Incident Command System (ICS) to systematically deal with almost any imaginable situation. After transitioning from law enforcement to the private sector, and working with numerous companies in a corporate security role, sadly, I have learned that most companies do not have a plan to deal with risks and emergency situations (the punch in the mouth) which could result in adverse or even devastating consequences to their employees and business. Many companies are focused on IT security as they should be, but have completely ignored physical security risks and have no plans to mitigate or deal with them.

My lifelong friend and colleague, Kevin Rice has identified this disconnect and has sought to assist organizational leaders by showing how basic law enforcement and threat assessment techniques can be utilized in the private sector. Businesses today simply cannot afford to operate without incorporating the tried and true basics of these concepts. The time to identify risks is not when a situation is happening. Hoping that something terrible could never happen is never a good strategy.

Kevin's career spans over three decades, and his organizational and operational experience is second to none. He has served as a police officer in Orlando, FL, and as a Special Agent with the United States' Secret Service. While with the Secret Service, Kevin held numerous positions including Special Agent, polygraph examiner, vice presidential protective detail agent, instructor at the Federal Law Enforcement Training Center (FLETC), Assistant to the Special Agent in Charge, Los Angeles Field Office, Assistant Special Agent in Charge, Little Rock Field Office, and Special Agent in Charge at the Phoenix Field Office. After transitioning to the private sector, Kevin was the Director of Asset Protection and Investigations for a multi-billion dollar company that operates in over ninety countries. Kevin is currently an Associate Director of Safety and Security at a university in Maine.

Kevin has distilled his vast knowledge and experiences into this much-needed resource for business leaders at all levels. He uses his unique style to communicate, to any organizational leader, to take the time-tested principles of risk mitigation from the law enforcement world, and adopt them into a workable plan for companies of any size. The time to act is now. Your employees deserve it and your company's future relies on it.

- Phil Carlson

Orange County Sheriff's Office, Orlando, FL, (Ret.)

U.S. Dept. of Homeland Security–FLETC (Ret.)

Things That Go Bump in the Night

From ghoulies and ghosties

And long-leggedy beasties

And things that go bump in the night,

Good Lord, deliver us!

Anonymous

ABOUT THE TITLE

As I thought about capturing the essence of this book with an appropriate title, I was comforted by two quotes attributed to business legend Arnold Glasow. His story is an American success story and I recommend that you read up on his life. The first Glasow quote struck me to the core because this book is fundamentally about training leaders, to prevent horrific acts before they happen. Glasow, a successful leader in his own right during the Great Depression, was once quoted as having said, "One of the tests of leadership is the ability to recognize a problem before it becomes an emergency." The entire premise of this book is summed up in that Glasow quote. This book is intended to provide you with the ability to recognize problems, specifically workplace violence before it rears its ugly head in your organization. The second Glasow quote, relevant to the contents of this book, discussed the fact that the future cannot be constrained and that leaders can't delay or postpone dealing with future problems. Although Glasow probably never envisioned workplace violence as an issue to be dealt with by today's leaders, it is still relevant. Glasow once stated that "The trouble with the future is that it usually arrives before we're ready for it."

This book aims to make you ready for the future, at least the future where you create a safer workplace.

There is a tendency of managers in all organizations to view scary (albeit rare) scenarios, such as targeted violence at work, like unicorns. The managers hope that due to the odds involved, they can ignore the situation and that workplace violence will not visit their organization. And as many speakers have said, hope is not a strategy. Or, many organizational leaders will pass this type the responsibility, of preparing for and taking proactive steps, to thwart workplace violence off to the HR or the security departments, and never concern themselves again with planning for such a rare possibility.

The title of this book has undergone several changes. I originally planned it to be called 'Cross-Pollination,' because I envisioned that the book would be able to pass concepts from one type of profession onto another. I then changed the title to 'Bumps in the Night,' alluding to the fact that all organizational leaders tend to concentrate on the business at hand and fail to concern themselves with issues like workplace violence until something goes bump in the night. I then flirted with incorporating something about waiting for the second shoe to drop. But then, I finally landed on the old saying- "Forewarned is Forearmed." It captured the core meaning of this book. The essence was the fact that I wished to warn and educate business leaders and HR personnel. I was confident that if I could inform these folks, they would incorporate relevant safety concepts, and together we might be able to save lives and increase productivity. I planned to take the best concepts from the two career fields I know best (law enforcement and threat assessment), and make it relevant to business and HR leaders.

Leaders know for a fact that some type of targeted violence event will eventually occur in their organization. Maybe it will be a small event, like a domestic violence incident involving married employees, or a fistfight between competing managers. Leaders hope and pray that it will not be anything worse than that. Leaders play the odds, and they hope that the other shoe never drops. But, with a little bit of education, leaders can now be better prepared if that bad day reaches their organization.

For those unfamiliar with the saying on which the title is based, here is what the internet says about it: "Advance warning provides an advantage. The Latin saying *'praemonitus, praemunitus'* loosely translates as 'forewarned is forearmed'."

So, the premise of the book is simple. I will provide, to organizational leaders, signs and clues that telegraph potential danger and provide them with tools to counter that danger. Hopefully, they use that warning to their advantage.

Targeted violence in the workplace, in my opinion, is an expected and inevitable event. You, as a manager, should lead before the other shoe drops. We hope that this book will empower you to make better decisions and plan more effectively on this subject.

ABOUT ME

I am the proud son of a New York police detective. My dad continues to be the smartest and most charismatic man I have ever met, and I have interacted with some fairly famous and powerful people in my life. After college, I wanted to follow in the footsteps of that great man, so I pursued law enforcement and spent thirty years in that profession. I started out as a police officer in Orlando, Florida, but spent the bulk of my entire adult life as a Special Agent with the United States Secret Service.

During the course of a very successful twenty-three-year tenure with the Secret Service, I held numerous positions in various locations. It was truly the honor of a lifetime to work among such professionals and play a small role in providing safe environments for several presidents, vice presidents, candidates, cabinet secretaries, foreign leaders, and miscellaneous other officials. Along the way, I was a firearms instructor, a criminal investigator, a threat assessor, and a polygraph examiner. I was promoted to several leadership positions within the Secret Service and was blessed with the opportunity to supervise some of the most talented and gifted law enforcement officers in the world, as well as a couple of knuckleheads (every organization has some).

At the tail end of my public sector experience, I left the Secret Service and was recruited to take a senior leadership position with another Federal law enforcement agency in the Intermountain West. Ultimately, I retired from federal law enforcement and took a security director position for a multi-billion-dollar company in the South. That is where, and when, I understood that leaders in the private sector see the world through very different lenses than the people I had been exposed to for the last thirty years. Their lenses were not wrong and they are perfect glasses to be worn when worrying about the bottom line. However, that vision often left them blind to some very obvious danger signs. Therefore, I knew that I needed to bring realistic training and life-saving concepts to the business world.

I am a member of the American Society of Industrial Security (ASIS), the International Law Enforcement Educators and Trainers Association (ILEETA), as well as numerous other law enforcement groups. Most importantly, for the themes associated with this book, I am a member and proponent of the Association of Threat Assessment Professionals (ATAP). I recently authored (along with co-author Phil Carlson) a book entitled *From Sheepdog to the C-Suite*, which was intended to assist law enforcement and military veterans transition to positions in corporate security. (Shameless plug alert: If you know a veteran or cop looking to transition to the private sector, we would be honored if they took a look at our book). I am currently working on a book of funny stories and experiences from my days as both a police officer and a Secret Service agent.

I am a graduate of the University of Central Florida with a BS in Criminal Justice. I graduated from Troy State University with a Master's degree in Public Administration, and I am also an alumnus of Northwestern University's School of Police Staff and Command. I am currently a security director for a small university in Maine. My wife Cynthia and I live on a small farm outside of Bangor, where we care for some rescue animals and we shovel lots of snow. When we moved to Maine, I was told there are three seasons, this winter, last winter, and next winter. They were not lying.

In addition to my day job, my friend Phil Carlson and I routinely speak to groups on varied subjects such as workplace violence, threat assessments, and a proactive mindset. We consult with corporations, and we train business leaders and HR professionals. We invite you to learn more by checking out our website at www.trustandconfidence.org If you like this book, you will love our live presentations.

We invite you to provide us with feedback. We'd love to hear from you. Feel free to drop me an email at trustandconfidencekr@gmail.com.

INTRODUCTION

"Some men were meant to be policemen; some were meant to be milkmen."

That sexist and antiquated (even then) statement was once spoken to me by a Captain in a police department when I was training an especially troubled young police recruit who wasn't cutting the mustard during his field training time. But the Captain was right, the nub of his proclamation was that everyone is cut out for specific work. You, the reader of this book, or at least the target audience of this book, are leaders in the business world or Human Resource fields. You excel at your chosen profession and you have no desire to be a cop or a threat assessor. And you have the respect of your author because you make organizations excel. You are the heart of our capitalistic society and you are the problem solvers. You didn't go to business school to learn to deal with violent people, nor do you want to deal with them. You didn't get into Human Resources to deal with threats in the workplace; I am sure you entered the HR field to assist people with career enhancement, benefits, and all the rest.

But, in today's current environment, organizations routinely have to worry about disgruntled employees, active shooters, stalkers, and threats of all kinds. If you are like most of the people leading organizations or coordinating HR resources, you have probably given scant attention to learning simple common-sensical tools to identify potentially violent employees, how to manage such situations, and, hopefully, prevent them in the first place.

Do you know who has that type of information? The people that learn to survive interacting with potentially violent human beings on a daily basis? Cops.

Do you know who, as part of their job, learns to identify threats, assess concerning behaviors, and manage those folks? Threat Assessors.

Cops and threat assessors, these are not the usual backgrounds of successful business leaders or HR professionals. But, people in the business world or HR fields would be wise to learn life skills and mindset from cops and threat assessors to survive and prosper in their careers. Especially in this age of workplace violence, active shooters, and litigation.

So, you are in luck, I have thirty years of law enforcement and threat assessment experience. This book represents information that my friend Phil Carlson and I have discussed, researched, and taught for a total of six decades. In addition to our lengthy careers in law enforcement, Phil and I also have fifteen years of combined experience in the corporate security field where we worked with senior leadership and the HR departments in preventing and de-escalating violence in the workplace. So, this book represents viewpoints unlike those you would routinely find in the real world. We are not your everyday cop on the beat, offering you anecdotal stories on how to prepare yourself for issues in the workplace. Not only have we walked a beat, been investigators, conducted hundreds of threat assessments (many of them were threats against the president of the United States), but we have held corporate security director positions for multi-billion-dollar companies. We know the corporate mindset and we know the legal, ethical, and moral tightrope that HR professionals walk on a daily basis. We know how to protect you from harm. Well, let me rephrase that, we know what to teach you in order to help you protect yourself...and this book attempts to accomplish that. We will present a series of concepts. Concepts that are designed to give you a basic knowledge and understanding of safety in the workplace. Like any other concept, it will be up to you on how to deploy it. Let me explain.

I know the concept of changing a tire.

I have read about the concept of changing a tire.

I have witnessed others perform the concept of changing a tire.

I, unfortunately, have even deployed the concept of changing a tire myself on several occasions.

But, like most concepts, I don't use it daily, but I know how to use it when I need to. That is what we will accomplish together in this book, we will teach you concepts.

Our goal is to take the experience we had as police officers, federal agents, and private sector security directors, and make it relevant and appropriate for leaders in business and Human Resources.

None of what we present here will be earth-shattering. Knowing how to correctly change a tire is not mind-blowing information either. But if you found yourself in a remote location, with temperatures dropping and snow starting to fall, and you hear that undeniable sound of your tire popping, there is no concept of greater importance to you, at that moment than knowing how to change that tire. It is the same in your organization. You, hopefully, will never need the concepts presented here. But I think you will sleep better knowing them and incorporating them into your work life. Knowing the tire changing concept doesn't make you a mechanic or a pit crew member. It makes you someone who, should the need arise, is better prepared to deal with that particular situation.

We are confident that after reading the book you will have a better understanding of the potential problems that can arise in organizations, and be equipped to identify the issues beforehand and, hopefully, minimize its consequences.

We are not striving to make you police officers, threat assessors, or even corporate security personnel. What we are doing is providing you tools, tools to better protect yourself and serve the employees in your care. You should not come out paranoid after reading the book. We will not make you believe that there is a killer secretly biding his or her time within your organization, ready to pounce. But we hope to prepare you for the probable and not only the possible.

So, how are we going to educate you on such matters? We have taken some of the most universal concepts used in police training, as well as some of the foundational precepts in the field of threat assessment, and have presented them buffet-style to you. Take what you want from this book and discard what you feel is not relevant. We aim not to make you subject matter experts on any of the subjects presented here, but to provide you with tools to deal with problematic and potentially violent employees or visitors.

You may choose your profession for a lot of reasons, but at the end of the day, you want to run a business so that you, your employees, and shareholders can all make some profit. If you are an HR representative, you are of an added value to both your organization and its employees. You do things, you create things, and you lead people. It's all about the business and making it better, more profitable, and beneficial. You go through life thinking about meetings, budgets, stock prices, shipments, and taxes. You concern yourself with production, advertising, marketing, grants, loans, insurance, turnover rates, and all the rest. After all, it's all about the business.

It's all about the business...until it isn't. It's all about the business until something goes bump in the night and the other shoe drops.

It's all about making those third-quarter earnings until a disgruntled employee returns to the workplace with a gun.

It's all about beating last month's manufacturing quotas until the CEO receives a note threatening her life.

It's all about ensuring that annual performance reviews are completed before the end of the physical year until a manager approaches you and says that employees are complaining that Fred in Accounting is acting strangely and has stopped bathing and brushing his teeth.

It's all about the creation and introduction of a new product line until your administrative assistant is being stalked by a guy she met online and she comes to you for guidance and protection.

It's all about your organization's positive social media image until two managers have a huge fistfight during the annual holiday party, and the video of those two nitwits goes viral.

You want to run a business or an HR department, you don't want to be a police officer, a threat assessor, or even a milkman.

You lead your organization with skill and acumen. The intent of the book is to make you more insightful, more talented, and better prepared.

The book will provide the latest concepts on how to prevent or positively react before the other shoe drops within your organization. After all, with you in your role, it's all about the business. Until it isn't!

SECTION ONE

FOREWARNED IS FOREARMED
(BECAUSE BAD THINGS DO HAPPEN TO GOOD ORGANIZATIONS)

CHAPTER ONE

"CROSS-POLLINATION"

At least weekly, if not daily, we hear about some event of workplace violence. Whether it is a domestic situation gone bad, a stalker, a disgruntled employee, or an act of terror, we have gotten used to hearing about violent acts taking place within the work environment. According to statistics from the Department of Labor, there were five hundred workplace homicides in 2016 and four hundred fifty-eight workplace homicides in 2017. According to the FBI, in a report titled "Active Shooter Incidents in the United States in 2018," there were twenty-seven active shooter incidents in sixteen states during the calendar year 2018. Those attacks resulted in eight-five deaths and one hundred twenty-eight people being wounded. The FBI reports that sixteen of those twenty-seven incidents occurred in areas of commerce, i.e. businesses. According to the Occupational Safety and Health Agency (OSHA), nearly two million American workers report having been victims of workplace violence each year. OSHA concedes that those numbers may be low because it believes that many cases of workplace violence go unreported (Lebron, 2019).

Here are some other frightening statistics I recently observed from a blog post written by Andrea Lebron. These statistics should concern any business leader or HR representative:

- Homicides make up nine percent of all deaths in the American workplace.
- The third leading cause of death in certain industries is attributed to workplace violence.
- For women in the workforce, workplace violence is the second leading cause of death while on the job.
- More bad news for women in the workplace, there are approximately thirty thousand reports of rapes and sexual assaults in the workplace annually.
- Organizations report one hundred and twenty-one billion dollars in annual losses directly attributable to workplace assaults.
- Domestic violence issues, that make its way into the workplace, cause seven hundred and twenty-seven dollars in lost productivity.
- Workplace catastrophic incidents, such as large-scale workplace violence, can cost publicly traded companies eight percent losses in shareholder value (Lebron, 2019).

An Associated Press article, written by Lisa Marie Pane and published in the last week of 2019, proclaimed, "U.S. Mass Killings Hit New High in 2019, Most Were Shootings." She cites a database compiled by several media companies, which showed a total of forty-one mass killings. Thirty-three of the forty-one mass killings were mass shootings. Pane writes that two-hundred and ten people were killed as a result of these events. She argues that a majority of the killings involved people that knew each other. The headline is confusing because in her article she writes that there were two hundred and twenty-four victims in 2017, many as a result of the horrible mass-shooting which took place in Las Vegas. In Pane's article, there is a quote that is consistent with the main theme of this book. The quote is "These are still rare events. Clearly, the risk is low but the fear is high. What fuels the contagion is fear" (Pane, 2019).

We could not agree more with the preceding quote. The odds that you, as an HR professional or organizational leader, will have to deal with an active shooter situation is quite rare. But you will, more than likely, deal with dozens of disgruntled employees and smaller workplace violence issues over the course of your career. But, with those active shooter numbers in mind, do you think the average CEO, mid-level manager, first-line supervisor, or HR professional has the requisite training and mindset to deal with the repercussions of a shooter or other types of workplace violence? I personally don't think so, based on my observations in the private sector. That is a sad state of affairs, especially since this is not a new phenomenon for the business and HR worlds.

Since the early 1970s, when OSHA was first created, there has been a "General Duty Clause" of the Occupational Safety and Health legislation. That clause states the following: "Each employer shall furnish to each of his employees employment, and a place of employment, which are free from recognized hazards that are causing or are likely to cause death or serious physical harm to his employees." [1]

It is clearly understood in civil actions and OSHA rulings that workplace violence is a recognized hazard that is likely to cause death or serious physical harm. So, isn't it of paramount importance to learn, as much as you can, about workplace violence and how to prevent it?

Who, in the business world, is expected to forecast this type of violent behavior?

Who is expected to protect the employees from these types of acts?

Who is forced to deal with the fallout from this violence?

The answers to those last three questions are:

---

1 https://www.osha.gov/laws-regs/oshact/section5-duties

- The senior leaders and middle managers of the company, and every member of the Human Resources department.

In other words, you, the reader of this book, are left to deal with the prevention of and reaction to these types of incidents. It is you who is expected to predict, deny, and otherwise address workplace violence. More often than not, your average supervisor or HR employee has had little or no training in the basic concepts that could help them survive such an event, or even better, prevent these types of situations. Human Resource employees, and other leaders, could greatly benefit from learning, understanding, and even embracing some elementary basics that are known and utilized by cops and threat assessors all over the United States. Providing these simple and commonsensical foundations and making them relevant to business leadership, and to the field of Human Resources, is the reason for this book.

This is not a book on physical self-defense in the workplace but instead concentrates on incorporating a mindset in the workplace.

Not paranoia, but preparation.

Not fear, but planning.

Not naivety, but an understanding of potential outcomes.

My friend and confidante Phil Carlson, a life-long police officer who is now a security director for a large corporation in North Carolina, tells his employees, that we should always plan for the probable and not the possible.

With the wrong mindset about all the potential issues in the workplace, managers or HR reps could find themselves overwhelmed and paralyzed. Being prepared for the probable though makes the leader much more confident. I just used the word 'leader,' and I did that for a purpose. Going forward in the book, if you see the word 'leader,' it will stand for anyone that might need to incorporate the lessons in this book, namely first-line supervisors, middle managers, senior executives, and especially HR personnel. So, when you read 'leader,' please know that I mean anyone in the workplace with the responsibility of representing an organization and interacting with other employees.

The art and science of management, and human resource management specifically, is a culture unto itself. Like other professions, it has its own professional organization, the Society of Human Resource Management (SHRM), it has its own language, its own culture, and its own legal requirements. In every way imaginable, the folks employed in the Human Resource (HR) and business administration fields are professionals. The subject matter experts in these career paths strive to follow best practices and to be fair and consistent in all of their endeavors. HR professionals and business leaders have learned much from other fields of study, and have incorporated input from those fields to better the field of their endeavors. I doubt I would get much disagreement if I stated that HR and business leaders have learned much from the legal profession, the medical profession, and from many of the social sciences.

But, in my opinion, and based on my observations of both public sector and private sector, I believe that it is time for HR folks and other workplace leaders to learn from the fields of law enforcement and threat assessment to create a safer environment for themselves and for the other employees they serve. As a career law enforcement officer, trainer, and threat assessor, I spent my entire adult life assessing risks and taking actions to create countermeasures against violent acts. So, it pains me to say that time and time again I have personally witnessed HR representatives engaging in activities that could make them, or others, embarrassed, injured, or even killed. As I have interacted with business leaders and HR professionals throughout the years, I have been shocked to see how ill-prepared, and I could argue naïve, these professionals have been when it comes to human nature, targeted violence, and ensuring a safe environment in the workplace. I know that the last statement might seem brash, and it is not my intent to denigrate or insult these people. The naivety and the failure to interpret potential threatening behavior, that I have witnessed in Human Resource personnel and business leaders, seems to be a result of their education, their culture, and the insular nature of their work. After all, HR professionals and business managers tend to be cliquish and for good reason. They operate in an environment where they have highly sensitive information about the personnel they serve and, from what I have seen, tend not to socialize with others outside of the HR or operational realm. I think HR professionals and senior organizational leadership are all highly aware that a friend in the workplace today could potentially be someone they have to discipline, suspend, or terminate tomorrow.

In many ways, HR professionals and leadership positions in the private sector have many similarities to cops, so why not look at that profession and see what positives can be gleaned from that field? Let me discuss, in bullet points, some of the commonalities between being a cop and working in Human Resources or business management:

- The higher purpose of both professions is to serve and safeguard the people they are responsible for.
- Both professions have strict rules that must be adhered to.
- Both professions are seen as the rule enforcers of that society, a necessary evil to ensure order and fairness.
- As mentioned earlier, both professions are siloed and insular.
- Both professions see people at their best and their worst.
- Both cops and HR professionals/business leaders make decisions that will positively or negatively impact people in fundamentally important and long-lasting ways.

- The general public often undervalues, misunderstands, and ridicules both professions.

- Popular culture often belittles both professions in TV, movies, and books.

- Both professions can be the target of rage and violence as a result of them carrying out their duties.

It is that last bullet point that forms the reason for this book to be written. This book is needed now more than ever and the business world needs to incorporate the basic concepts outlined in the following pages in order to increase their odds at detecting and/or preventing violent acts in the workplace. So, if human resources and business administration as professions have much in common with law enforcement, why shouldn't these leaders at least look to any successes that law enforcement has had, especially as it relates to identifying, assessing, and managing potential threats. It is the major premise of this book that leaders have much to learn from the criminal justice field and that your authors are uniquely qualified, based on our background and experience, to present it.

There are a dozen or so basic concepts that are universal truths for cops and threat assessment professionals, and they are directly relevant to anyone who is employed in HR or business.

This book will present a series of law enforcement and threat assessment concepts that are ubiquitous in police academies throughout the United States and the world but are probably foreign ideas to the vast majority of people employed in the private sector. Our goal for this book is to present these concepts, define them, but most importantly show its relevance to the business arena. But if you ask us what we really want to accomplish with this book, we would tell you that we never again want to see an HR employee or business leader do something unsafe or unwise. We hope that this book finds a following in the business and HR world, and it creates honest reflection and a resolution to examine what law enforcement and threat management perspectives might offer to the profession.

Now, don't get me wrong, even with all the similarities mentioned in the bullet points above, I am fully aware that the fields of law enforcement/threat assessment have more differences than similarities with the world of business/human resources. I won't insult you by listing how business leaders and law enforcement people are entirely foreign to each other. This book is not intended to make HR professionals and business leaders into cops or professional threat assessors, but I think there is an opportunity to use philosophically sound officer safety techniques and threat assessment concepts in the business world to reduce workplace violence and create safer work environments.

CHAPTER TWO

"WHY LISTEN TO ME?"

The preceding chapter outlined the need and justification for publishing this book. Hopefully, you are willing to approach the following chapters with an open mind. Hopefully, you find some insights that will assist you in your role of leading people in the private sector, but why should you listen to a word that I have to say?

When writing this book, I bounced ideas and concepts off of Phil Carlson. I wanted his experience and expertise to keep me grounded and to ensure that I was not straying from best business practices. Phil lists his background and experience in the "Foreword" of this book. I am honored to call Phil Carlson a life-long friend and I am blessed that he has contributed to this book. His feedback and insight made this a better book than I could have ever written if left to my own devices.

As for me, let me make an admission against interest. I am not a Human Resource professional, and I don't possess an MBA. I am not a member of SHRM. I have never taken a Human Resources course at any college or university. So why do I have the nerve to attempt to teach well trained and highly professional HR subject matter experts and business leaders anything?

Well, that answer is simple. After thirty years in law enforcement and threat assessment, I retired from the public sector and was hired by a multi-national corporation as a Security Director. I brought with me to the private sector all of my experiences as a city cop, a Secret Service agent, a polygraph examiner, a threat assessor, and a public sector manager. I brought with me the experiences of personally witnessing deception, rage, senseless violence, and actions by sociopaths, psychopaths, and mentally ill individuals. As fate would have it, in my role in the corporate sector, my physical office space as Security Director was located within the HR department. I also dotted line reported to the Senior VP of Human Resources. At first, the HR employees didn't know how to take the presence of this retired cop/agent in their department. But I laid low and took my time. I helped where I could but I tried to stay in my lane.

In that role, I personally witnessed, on a daily basis, the work that is done by HR professionals. I watched the HR team work with waves upon waves of employees and I came away impressed by the jack of all trades that an HR professional has to be. I watched as every employee that walked through the

HR doors had a unique question, complaint, or request. I saw these employees at their highest points when they were promoted, acknowledged, or given raises, and I saw dozens, if not hundreds, of counseling sessions, suspensions, and terminations. I saw employees filled with rage and venom, and I saw employees cry with joy. But what I also saw, at least once a day, was an HR employee do something that was inherently and unintentionally unsafe or unwise. I saw managers and HR employees place themselves physically or psychologically at a disadvantage. I watched them give the upper hand to potentially violent employees, and it concerned me immensely. I would offer advice where I could. I always tried to downplay the advice and minimize anything that made me sound paranoid or overzealous. What I found, as I worked daily within the HR department, is that these HR professionals were not committing these unsafe acts intentionally, it was just that no one had ever walked them through some basic concepts that are drilled into cops and federal agents from their first hour on the job.

So, again I ask, "Why should any HR professional or business leader listen to me about this subject matter?"

In an attempt to convince the reader that I have experience and expertise in officer safety, threat assessment, workplace violence, crime prevention, and a myriad of other skill-sets regarding the subject matter of this book, I offer you a snapshot of my career, education, and mind-set. There is some hesitance in listing my resume here because this book is not about me. It's about you and your organization. Mostly, it's about keeping you and your people safe by creating a new way of looking at your work environment. But in order to do that, I need you to trust me and trust the fact that I know what I am talking about.

I am the first person to admit that I am not an American hero. I do not possess the physical strength or willpower of your average U.S. Marine, I don't have the brains or acumen of a fighter pilot. I am not as brave as the firefighter at your nearest firehouse, and I could never be a surgeon or an ER nurse for a multitude of reasons. I don't have the patience of a teacher. The people in those professions are true American heroes, and I thank them for the selfless devotion to their community and country. But, I have been exposed to certain training and work assignments that make me an expert on creating safe environments for people. So, please read my background information in the vein that I intend it, which is to convince you that on the subject matters in this book, I have credibility. But that is ultimately for you to decide.

When discussing my experience, I guess I have to start with how I was raised and the seeds that were sown by my upbringing. My father, who was my childhood hero, was a New York City police detective. I watched him, on a daily basis, use his acquired talents to detect deception, deescalate angry people, and understand human behavior. I witnessed him take a path in which violence was always the last resort. I saw my two brothers also enter law enforcement, and I watched them transform and become better at spotting liars, predicting violent behavior, and using their communication skills to calm down highly enraged people.

I went to college and majored in criminal justice and political science. While attending college, I worked as a loss prevention officer for a national department store. In that job, I had my first true dose of reality when it comes to human behavior. I watched people for a living, oftentimes from behind two-way mirrors or from a distance to avoid detection. I saw consistent behaviors demonstrated by people before they stole items, saw a different set of behaviors while they were stealing, and witnessed their almost universal actions as they tried to cover their tracks and escape the store. I listened to their denials when I confronted them and I heard their lies. Many times, I had to chase them as they attempted to run from their guilt, literally and figuratively. I also, unfortunately, had dozens of these shoplifters use violence against me. I got to see rage up close and personal, and I learned to use my wits to attempt to calm the situation.

After graduating from college, I was hired by the Orlando Police Department as a police officer. During the four-month police academy, there was one underlying principle bubbling under the surface of every subject matter we were taught. That principle was that of officer safety, and there were a million ways to make every call to which you responded or every traffic stop that you initiated into a safer one. Much of what was taught had to do with listening to people (what they were saying and more importantly, not saying), watching body language, and putting yourself in their shoes. After completing the police academy, I underwent, like every other cop, an extensive field training program, usually called "FTO" in law enforcement parlance. During this training program, I rode with and was evaluated by four different training officers for a total of around eighty days. Each training officer taught me much about human nature, the precursors of violence, and how best to attempt to deflate highly charged emotions.

I spent four years as a police officer, operating in the worst neighborhoods in the city of Orlando. Neighborhoods where I literally saw or touched crack cocaine or some other illicit drug on a daily basis. Every day, many of the people I interacted with either lied to me, ran from me, or attempted to fight me. Some people did all three things. My experience was not unique. Every other officer I knew experienced the same events daily. In my last year on OPD, I was a field training officer and had a dozen of young recruits assigned to ride with me to be trained. My goal, when training them, was to always ensure their safety and I discussed many of the concepts in this book with those young officers.

But, my lifelong dream was to always be a Secret Service agent. I achieved that dream after my four-year stint on OPD. Once hired by that storied federal agency, I underwent eight months of training at two separate training academies, the Federal Law Enforcement Training Center and the Special Agent Training Course at the Secret Service Training Academy in Beltsville, Maryland. During a very successful twenty-three year career as a special agent in the Secret Service, I was placed in dozens of positions that taught me much about the subjects we will discuss in this book. These types of experiences would be extremely helpful to your average HR employee or business leader. The following points can be helpful more specifically:

- I was responsible for investigating hundreds of threats against presidents, vice presidents, and other secret service protected persons. In each threat case, I interviewed the person making the threat. That type of experience is invaluable in understanding grievances, pre-attack behaviors, threat making, and many times, mental health issues.

- I underwent specialized training given by the Department of Defense to become certified as a federal polygraph examiner. As a Secret Service polygraph examiner for four years, I administered hundreds of polygraph exams to all sorts of criminals, persons of interest in intelligence cases, and applicants for jobs within the Secret Service. During these hundreds of exams, I was required to interview or interrogate anyone that the test revealed was deceptive to the test questions.

During the thousands of hours that I spent face to face with thugs, threat makers, and applicants, my job was to obtain ground truth from these people. I learned much about the way people lie and attempt to cover it up. I learned much about rage, self-preservation, and human frailties.

- During my time protecting our nation's leaders in the Secret Service, I scanned crowds, monitored body language, and looked for baselines and anomalies of the people in close proximity to the protectees. I learned to read visual cues from people and make instantaneous decisions on whether they meant harm to the people we were trying to protect. When working the inner perimeter security ring around our protectees, I could tell within a second if someone, fifty yards away, was going to cause a problem or not. I was not singularly gifted with this talent, almost every secret service agent I knew (after some experience) was able to do the same.

- I spent three years as a detailed instructor at the Federal Law Enforcement Training Center (FLETC) where it was now my turn to teach the latest techniques to young trainees, always reinforcing many of the concepts you will be exposed to further on in this book. Every instructor that I had the pleasure to work alongside had one goal, impart the trainees with foundational principles that they could use every day to potentially save their life. At FLETC, we referred to these principles as tools that the trainees could place in their toolbox. As in auto mechanics or carpentry, professionals don't use every tool on every job, but he/she should know how each tool works and when to use it.

- After my time at FLETC was through, I was fortunate enough to be promoted to three separate management positions within the Secret Service. In my first leadership position, I was a first-line supervisor of agents and civilians in a large field office. I supervised, on average ten to fifteen people, and got my first taste of how complicated humans can be to manage. In reality, though, I was fortunate. I was blessed with some outstanding people to lead. It was a great introduction to HR issues. My second management position was as second-in-command of a smaller office whose jurisdiction covered an entire state. In this office, I had a fantastic boss and administrative staff but I had to deal with some problematic young agents. Again, it prepared me to discuss troublesome employees with HR professionals. In my last assignment, I was a special agent in charge of all secret service operations in a two-state region, and I was ultimately responsible for all HR matters within the district.

- During my last two years as a federal employee, I had the opportunity to be a special agent in charge of another federal law enforcement agency in a four-state region of the western United States. The employees of this agency were all public-sector union employees, which was a departure for me from the secret service. The union in this agency was combative at every turn and created drama and controversy wherever it went. But it also made me much better versed in discussing the concepts in this book.

- Upon retiring from active law enforcement, I took up a position as a Security Director for a multi-national company, where I physically sat in the Human Resources department and personally witnessed what HR professionals experienced on a daily basis. In that role, I was a member of the company's threat assessment team and I provided training to managers and HR employees on workplace violence, risk assessment, and physical security.

- In my role in the private sector, I became a member of, and have attended specialized training courses offered by, the Association of Threat Assessment Professionals (ATAP). For more information on ATAP, I would ask you to visit their website at https://www.atapworldwide.org/

- As I write this book, I am an associate director of safety and security at a private college in Maine. My role is to ensure a safe environment for all of the students, faculty, and staff at the institution. In this current job, I partner with Human Resources about problematic employees (luckily, we don't have many), and I partner with various deans about students of concern. Lastly, I partner with our local law enforcement agencies regarding issues of potential threats from outsiders to our campus. I use the concepts described in this book every day. I find them powerful tools; I hope that you will too.

So, with those experiences in mind, I hope that you will now be convinced that I am uniquely qualified to discuss the main premise of this book, and that is, that HR professionals and organizational leaders could benefit from the lessons learned from cops and threat assessors.

CHAPTER THREE

"WHY WRITE THE BOOK NOW?"

Whether you like to think about it or not, if you are an HR professional or a leader in the business field, there are people looking to test you, on a daily basis, to get what they want. Many of these tests are minor in nature and would never involve physical violence, intimidation, or threats. But I want you to ask yourself this question: When that employee does resort to real or perceived violent acts, are you prepared to deal with it?

Are you mentally prepared to always place yourself in a position of advantage?

Do you incorporate the physical makeup of your surroundings to ensure your safety and the safety of those in your charge?

Do you know the difference between hunters and howlers?

Do you know what differentiates cover and concealment?

Do you treat terminations like the explosive situation it can be?

If you found yourself wondering about your responses to those last questions, don't feel bad. You are in the same boat as many other HR personnel and other business leaders.

So, why did we write this book? Simply put, we felt the need to offer up some real-world advice to the leaders in the private sector. We needed to teach concepts not discussed in business school or at HR seminars. Again, the concepts we will touch on are not based on paranoia. You can read this book and incorporate the concepts you find rational and no one will ever see any difference in your work style. When I listed my experiences in the last chapter, you read that I have known and experienced the concepts discussed in this book for years. So, why did I choose this specific time to write the book? That's an easy one. About a week before I cracked open the laptop to start this book, I had observed four separate incidents, all within the span of a few days of each other, which caused me grave concern. These incidents were created by leaders within my organization and caused me concern for my safety, concern for the safety of the HR personnel involved, and concern for the safety of all of the other employees in the building. Within forty-eight hours, I personally observed the below mentioned unwise and unsafe acts, all committed by senior leadership. Several of the people committing these actions were employees purporting to be highly trained HR personnel.

Here's what I saw:

- As a security director, I was briefed about the behavior of a particular employee and the ramifications of his actions, and I was requested to be on stand-by for his termination. Specifically, a middle-aged married male employee, let's call him Fred in Accounting, sought out the services of a woman I suspected to be a female prostitute. The female in question found out that our employee was married and she attempted to blackmail him. When our employee refused to give in to the blackmail attempts, the prostitute began a campaign of endless calls to our switchboard and also made threats to visit our employee at work and home. The prostitute ended up presenting photographic evidence of the employee's indiscretion to his wife. The wife visited our workplace and made a scene.

  HR made the decision to terminate the employee. The employee had been known to me as a braggart and I believed him to be a serial liar. He often tried to convince me that he was a former federal agent and had conducted secret missions on behalf of the US government. I had all sorts of reservations that this employee might become problematic and discussed my concerns with the HR professionals handling the matter. I initiated a plan to counter any potential acts by the employee. I stressed de-escalation to the HR employee, and they agreed to leave the employee with as much pride and respect as they could.

As the HR employee terminated him in a small office near the exit door, all went well. I had positioned myself just outside that office in case anything bad started happening. As the termination meeting was concluding, I watched as a very senior leader in our organization walked into the room, spoke to the employee for a few seconds, and then began to leave the room. Instead of face-saving and soft-shoeing the termination to ensure a peaceful departure, this supposed leader looked at the employee and literally said, "This is what you get when you make poor life decisions," the "leader" then turned around and exited the room.

So much for de-escalation and face-saving!

Luckily, for me, the terminated employee was more ashamed than insulted and left without any issue. Well, except for throwing some paperwork on the parking lot asphalt and burning rubber in his vehicle as he drove away. But I shudder in fear when I think about the impact that that one sentence could have had on the employee's mental state, and what it could have sparked in him. I shake my head when I think that a "senior leader" in the organization could make such an asinine statement in that environment.

I knew that I had to write a book that discussed the gravity of termination on an employee's psyche, and the fact that termination is a significant life stressor and that those significant life stressors are found in almost every act of mass shooting or targeted violence.

- In the second incident, I was speaking with a senior leader at my workplace who was genuinely concerned about his safety, and the safety of others as a result of an employee's (let's call him Fred from Accounting) recent actions. The second the leader mentioned Fred's name, I immediately recognized it, even though there are one thousand employees in that particular facility.

Fred's actions and his behavior had always been on my radar as an employee with potential anger management issues, although it was never anything that I could quantify. The leader then described to me a recent interaction that he and Fred's first-line manager had with the employee and my concerns deepened.

Specifically, Fred had recently become interested in a married female employee with a history of office romance issues. As a result of Fred's new love interest, both his and her work had suffered. As such, the senior leader discussed Fred's actions with the HR and a decision to start verbal counseling was made.

A meeting was held with Fred, Fred's first-line manager, and this senior leader. The meeting was professional, low key, and factual. During the meeting, the two managers laid out the facts and verbally counseled Fred to devote less time to social interaction and more time on his assigned work.

As disciplinary actions go, it was fairly innocuous and minimalist in nature, at least for a while.

As the managers finished the meeting, Fred stood up from his seat, while the two managers remained seated (psychologically that is significant). Fred looked at both managers individually, pointed at them, and declared in a loud voice, "You're yellow and you're yellow." Fred, visibly angry, left the meeting room abruptly and returned to work. Fred then authored a letter of resignation with an effective date of two weeks and submitted it to his first-line supervisor.

For someone to get that angry over verbal counseling, and then spitefully tender his resignation, should raise red flags and should be a cause for concern. The fact that he now had two weeks to sabotage the workplace was also a potential issue.

Both managers felt that Fred was potentially violent and was, at the least, disrespectful and insubordinate during the counseling decision.

After Fred departed the session, the two leaders went to Human Resources, explained the situation, and sought guidance on what actions to take in response to the insubordination in the meeting.

This was the HR's response: Just ignore Fred's actions, it wasn't violent in nature. He'll be gone in two weeks.

One of the two leaders (the more senior leader) came to me and shared his fear about this employee. I had never before seen this leader so worried. He was in fear of his life, and the other manager's life, and he worried that the employee might do something else like intentionally break a million-dollar piece of equipment or sabotage the company's records before the resignation went into effect.

I listened to the leader explain the situation and I offered my opinion in return. I explained that our company prided itself on a zero-tolerance policy on all types of workplace violence. I informed the senior leader that Fred's physical actions and his choice of words were violent by their very nature. (I will discuss a concept, called pre-assault indicators, later in the book), and I argued to the leader that Fred's actions were intended to instigate violence. I could articulate, rather effectively I think, that Fred's physical and verbal acts were a clear violation of the company's policy and needed to be addressed.

I advised the senior leader that due to the employee's written resignation, the fact that the employee had shown violent propensities, the fact that Fred had grievances against his managers, and that he had made up his mind to leave the company, we needed to convince the HR manager to terminate Fred immediately. I advised the senior leader that it was potentially problematic to allow Fred to remain in the workplace. I suggested asking HR to off-board the employee immediately but to continue to pay him through the date of his resignation. To many in the HR and business fields, this solution is called a "soft landing."

Luckily, HR management reversed their initial decision and listened to the concerns of the leader as he expressed, in his own words, my opinion of the seriousness of the issues at hand. HR changed their initial opinion based on these arguments and released Fred that day without incident. HR was able to soft-sell the departure as being good for him, i.e. allowing him to be paid while making the transition to a new job.

The HR management team, initially, was unwilling to see the potential for violence, disruption, and sabotage that this problematic employee could unleash. They were too comfortable in their own definition of what workplace violence is. It took a cop's mindset, and a threat assessor's experience to realize that Fred in Accounting was a potential time bomb and left to his own devices for two weeks could potentially explode all over the workplace.

So, HR was provided with another fresh perspective: 'Give two week's pay and get him out of the building. Make it positive for him.'

Two week's pay!

Two week's pay...what a small price to pay for safety; a small price to ensure that a potentially violent employee could not sabotage the workplace or have access to committing violence at work.

I know that there are some people out there who would say that we rewarded bad behavior. We gave two week's salary to someone who was insubordinate and belligerent. No one more than me hates the fact that this knucklehead walked out that day with two weeks of free salary, but I have to look at this rationally and not emotionally.

So what? What if Fred departed feeling that he had won, that he had defeated us? Who cares that he can sit in his recliner, drinking Bud Light for the next 14 days and collect a paycheck to boot? Compare that small amount of money to the havoc he could have unleashed on the corporation, its managers, and its employees. The value we received for that two-week paycheck was immeasurable.

That incident reinforced to me that I needed to write a book that detailed what pre-assault indicators are, and how these indicators might manifest themselves in the workplace. If business leaders and HR representatives don't have real-world experience about violent acts and how they start, how can they honestly attempt to enforce zero-tolerance policies? Hopefully, after reading this book, private sector leaders would look at Fred's words and actions in a different light.

- The third incident, I witnessed, occurred when I was asked to assist an HR manager with the termination of a senior leader in the organization. This senior leader was a scientist (and actually was not Fred from Accounting) and was, let me say this politically correctly, an odd duck. The leader had trouble with interpersonal relationships, and because of the employee's quirky personality, I had no idea how she would handle a termination. The HR personnel involved did not seek out advice from me on the off-boarding, and I was given the time and location of the off-boarding and was asked to be nearby when the termination took place.

Instead of conducting the termination in the usual location, which is in the HR department on the first floor, near the exit doors, I was asked to meet the HR manager on the second floor in the farthest distant corner in the building, surrounded by a dozen other offices and a hundred cubicles.

The HR manager met with the leader and conducted the termination. Now, the bad part. The HR manager and the terminated employee now had to walk the entire length of the second floor with the security director in tow in order to leave the building. Talk about embarrassment and loss of face, especially for someone with a Ph.D. after their name.

But, it gets worse.

Because HR had not thought this whole thing through, the HR manager now had a decision to make. Do I walk down a flight of stairs with an employee who just received some very bad news or do I accompany them in a very small elevator for the ride downstairs?

There is no good answer to that question.

Both are bad options. There had been no tactical or strategic decision-making by HR when the decision was made to conduct the termination in the scientist's own office.

When they were met with the stairs or elevator dilemma, I believe that is when the light came on for that particular HR manager. From my perspective, both the stairs and the elevator are very dangerous positions to voluntarily place yourself, especially when you have a perfectly good conference room that is very private and just a few feet from the exit doors. In a room like that, you could increase safety while simultaneously offering the terminated employee some privacy.

What did the HR leader do? They chose to use the elevator. I made the decision that I would use the stairs and meet them in the lobby when they got there. There was no sense in the three of us getting trapped inside an elevator with a potentially problematic employee.

Again, we were fortunate that in that particular termination, the employee did not become violent. But stop for a second and imagine what if the employee had become violent. What if that employee had become violent upstairs in the sea of cubicles, or on the stairs, or in the elevator?

The images evoked by that question are not good. Who in their right mind would make a decision to off-board someone in such an illogical and unsafe location as the distant corner of a second floor, and make your terminated employee take the walk of shame through a cubicle farm for five minutes? Then, accompany your terminated employee in the very uncomfortable setting of an elevator or a steep staircase, and then parade your off-boarded employee through the first floor.

How much credibility did the entire HR department lose by terminating a person and then escorting that person throughout the building for ten minutes? How many employees felt embarrassed for the terminated employee and felt more allegiance to the scientist than to the HR employee? Now I work for a leader whose goal for my current department is to constantly be "building bank," in other words, constantly creating goodwill. That HR termination failed to build any bank with anyone involved or anyone who witnessed it, including me.

The absurdity of this particular off-boarding and the decisions behind it literally caused me to lay awake that night. The next day, I scheduled a meeting with the HR leadership to troubleshoot the termination. As I expressed my concerns to the most senior HR leader at the facility, he became defensive and felt insulted that I questioned his decision. He looked me in the eyes and said that he had made the decision as to the location of the termination himself. He stated that he wanted to have the termination take place in the off-boarded employee's office "out of respect," and that he "can read people," and that he knew the "employee was not the type to commit violence."

When I heard those words, coupled with my knowledge that there is no profile of an active shooter, that there is no profile of people who commit workplace violence, I knew that this book needed to be written. I was befuddled by this HR leader's arrogance, lack of common sense, and more importantly his lack of survival skills for himself, his employees, and the workforce in general. I knew that there was no way that I could convince this leader that he was naïve toward human nature. It was at that exact minute that the seeds of this book were sown.

- The last scenario I observed, that caused me to author this book, is a short one. Maybe because of the HR leader's naiveté, one of his employees asked one of the members of my security team to provide a short briefing on conducting safe terminations. My employee provided a thorough briefing and as part of the orientation discussed the physical configuration of a room, especially as it relates to seating and the ability to access an exit quickly in the event of an emergency. My security specialist suggested where the HR representative should sit, where the first-line manager should sit, and where the soon to be terminated employee should sit. The security specialist ensured the room contained no items that could be easily used as a weapon and that the panic button in the interview room worked properly.

The HR employee handling the termination set the room up accordingly to ensure the safety of all involved when the first-line manager appeared with the employee in question. The first-line manager did not meet with the HR representative first and establish a game plan. The first-line supervisor allowed the off-boarded employee to sit where they wanted, thereby completely disrupting the security plan.

These four scenarios are symbolic of the fact that our business leaders and our HR folks are often very intelligent people who are learned in many subject matters but, they seem to lack a basic understanding of the concepts of safety and security. I believe that the basic tenets of law enforcement and threat assessment could prove very beneficial for business leaders and HR professionals.

It is for situations like those mentioned above, and hundreds of others I witnessed in the private sector, that this book had to be written.

CHAPTER FOUR

"THE PROBLEM OF WORKPLACE VIOLENCE"

This book is not intended to discuss the causes and reasons as to why the workplace can be a dangerous space. I hope that all managers, leaders, and HR professionals can see that as self-evident. Instead, I am working from the premise that if we are all in agreement, then let's look at instilling a proper survival and preparation mindset. But, before we delve into the concepts that leaders should know, to better prepare for issues at the job site, let's discuss the extent of the problem of workplace violence, why it happens, and what some triggers are.

As I mentioned in my bio, my father was an NYPD detective and he investigated and successfully closed many homicides, several of them fairly famous or infamous during their time. In my youth, I heard my father talk about how most homicides are not really whodunits, but, in fact, are quite easy to solve. He stated that many murder victims are killed by the people closest to them. He said that the first persons he wanted to interview during any homicide investigation were the people in the victim's most immediate social circle (spouses, children, parents, lovers, business partners, etc.). More often than not, the homicide was not committed by some robber, burglar, or a complete stranger. Instead, the majority of homicides, he stated, were committed by someone very emotionally and physically close to the victim. I guess that is how human nature has been since the days of Cain and Abel.

Why should the workplace be any different? Many times, we spend more hours of our day with our work family than we do with our home family. We get jealous of co-workers, we are ashamed of co-workers, we get insulted by co-workers, and we develop crushes on co-workers. We sometimes engage in sexual relationships with co-workers. Important to the subject at hand, we sometimes develop grievances against our fellow employees. Certain employees will stalk unrequited love in the workplace, and sometimes employees will seek revenge against those whom they see as hurdles in their success. If a husband can kill a wife, or a son kills his mother, is there any doubt that, with all of the emotions that take place at a job site, an employee couldn't kill, stalk, injure, or rape their co-worker or manager? We, as leaders in management or HR, need to prepare for the probable and not the possible.

I just mentioned emotions in the workplace. Before we look at some statistics about workplace violence, let's examine what work is and what it provides, solely from a layman's perspective, and by keeping the professionals out of the discussion for a minute. I would ask you, the reader, to answer these next questions silently and do some soul searching before reading further:

- What does my job mean to me?

- What do I receive psychologically from my job?

- How much of my self-identity is obtained through my job?

- How much of my mental, physical, and financial well-being is derived from my work?

- What would happen if I lost my job right now?

- What would I do if I thought someone was trying to sabotage me at work?

- Is there someone at my job that I do not trust, do not like, and want to see fail?

- Is there someone at work, that I could see myself having a serious long-term relationship with?

If you have answered these questions thoughtfully and took some time to think of the implications of the answers, it is evident that violence can erupt in the workplace. I read a recent article written by Rebecca Harrington entitled "The Nine Reasons Why People Snap, according to a Neurobiologist." The article appeared on the 'Business Insider' website. In the article, Harrington discusses the findings of neurobiologist R. Douglas Fields as outlined in his book *Why We Snap: Understanding the Rage Circuit in Your Brain*.

In that article, Harrington lists the nine triggers of rage. Specifically, Fields discusses the nine trigger points that means so much to us, that people will get filled with rage in order to defend it. As I list the nine triggers of rage, think about how many of those triggers can be associated with the workplace, especially with the loss of a job.

Harrington lists Field's triggers as:

- Being placed in a life or death situation
- Being insulted
- Protecting your family
- Protecting your "territory," i.e., your home
- Protecting your mate
- Protecting your social status
- Protecting valuables, such as money and other resources
- Protecting your "tribe"
- To escape being captured or restrained

In the article by Harrington, the reader gets the impression that many of these trigger points have been learned over thousands of years, and is a result of survival skills developed over a very long time. This need to defend ourselves from certain threats seems to be in our genes. As I look at the nine triggers, I can articulate at least five of the nine trigger points that can routinely appear in a workplace setting. In the right circumstances, I could articulate all nine of the trigger points occurring in a work environment.

So, if you are a leader in the workplace, you should always see how your actions may potentially be seen, by your subordinates or co-workers, through the lens of these trigger points. For example, you decide to demote someone and as a result, decrease their pay, does the affected employee see that demotion as a threat to their social status, a threat to their family, or an insult?

Do they see it as all three? That is why I offer these very basic concepts from law enforcement and threat assessment to the reader. These concepts, individually or collectively, can assist you in creating a safer workplace. They might just save your life or the life of a co-worker.

During the week that I wrote this chapter, the news on cable TV and the internet were filled with two stories of revenge committed by disgruntled employees at their respective places of employment. The first story centered on the judicial sentencing of a former employee who "doxed" a co-worker because he disagreed with their actions in the workplace. More specifically, the employee used his position to find personal information, like phone numbers, residential addresses, and the like, of his co-workers and placed that private information on websites to somehow seek vengeance upon them. The second incident involved a municipal worker in Virginia Beach who resigned via email to his boss and then drove to work and killed twelve co-workers and injured four more.

And, as I literally write this paragraph aboard a flight from North Carolina to Maine, I am reading a breaking news story about an employee of an automobile dealership in California who was terminated, and upon being fired, returned to the dealership and shot former co-workers and then shot himself. But we don't need these examples to reinforce what we, as organizational leaders and as HR employees, already know. Workplace violence happens and most of the time there are warning signs. We as leaders, first-line supervisors, and HR professionals can't place our heads in the sand. We need to operate with a different perspective, with the mindset of a sheepdog and not a sheep.

For too long we, as leaders, have operated from the mindset that the threat is exaggerated. We have also thought that we could learn from many experts in many fields but that there was NOTHING that law enforcement can teach us about mindsets. And most leaders don't even have a firm grip on what threat assessment really is and, therefore, do not believe that the fundamental operating ideas of threat assessment can assist them in their duties. When we speak about violence in this book, we are speaking about all types of targeted violence, not just active shooters. Although we will cite certain statistics in the book that discusses mass shootings or active shooter situations, we concern ourselves with any act of violence that takes place in the workplace.

As the FBI states in a report, "Violence can be categorized in one of two ways: predatory/planned violence or impulsive/reactive violence. The former is premeditated and serves some purpose for those who plan and conduct violent attacks. Impulsive/reactive violence, on the other hand, is emotional and impromptu; it is frequently a defensive behavior in response to a perceived imminent threat. These two types of violence are distinctively different," (U.S. Department of Justice, 2017). By and large, the violence that this book will concern itself with is the predatory/planned type.

The statistics expose the extent of the problem. As I mentioned earlier, an article by Andrea Lebron entitled "The Latest on Workplace Violence Statistics" lists some very discouraging but enlightening statistics on this subject matter.

Lebron states:

- Homicides make up nine percent of all causes of death in the workplace.
- That two million workers in the United States become workplace violence victims annually.

- For half of the population, women, workplace violence is the second leading cause of death in the workplace.

- There are thirty thousand acts of rape and sexual assault annually in the workplace.

In April 2020, the FBI released its report of active shooter incidents that took place within the United States, during the calendar year 2019. This report documented twenty-eight active shooter incidents in the U.S. in 2019. Those attacks caused two hundred and forty-seven casualties, with ninety-seven deaths and one hundred and fifty injuries. The vast majority of those attacks, almost half, in fact, took place in an area of commerce. In the grand scheme of things, twenty-eight mass attacks during the course of a year, in a country of three hundred and thirty million people, make these incidents rare (thankfully). But, as a manager, remember that the "active shooter" is only one type of targeted violence.

With Lebron's and the FBI's startling statistics in mind, we set off to learn some concepts that are universally used in law enforcement and threat assessment but are not part of the vernacular in the halls of business or HR interview rooms. Not yet anyway.

Let's get to it!

SECTION TWO

THE CONCEPTS

CHAPTER FIVE

"WHAT LAW ENFORCEMENT CAN TEACH BUSINESS LEADERS AND HR EMPLOYEES"

There are about a million law enforcement officers employed in the United States by approximately 18,000 different agencies. These folks are employed by municipal police departments, county sheriff's offices, state police agencies, and federal agencies. Our founders wanted the police powers of the United States decentralized and feared the presence of one large enforcement agency. As a radio talk show host, whom I listen to often, says and I paraphrase here, 'the larger the government the smaller the citizen.' So, we have a quilt of small police agencies with one or two employees and we have large city departments like NYPD with tens of thousands of police officers. All of these agencies have written their own policies and procedures, and all rely on their own training units or training officers to impart information to their agency employees. So, with thousands of different agencies out there, you would envision that there would be a huge variation in the concepts taught to officers or agents to instill officer survival skills and develop a mindset where they see the world differently than their fellow citizens. But based on my experience, I can confidently state that the concepts that are about to be outlined on the following pages are almost universal. These concepts provide officers with confidence and a blueprint from which to operate in many uncertain circumstances.

Based on thirty years in law enforcement, fifteen years as a senior manager leading people, and my time working hand in hand with HR personnel and other leaders, I can be unequivocal in the following statement:

'Managers, senior leaders, and HR personnel would be wise to examine the basic tenets of law enforcement and threat assessment and put these concepts in perspective about the jobs they perform and where appropriate, incorporate these survival concepts into their own workplaces.'

In the following pages of this section, I will introduce ideas from the world of law enforcement, explain the concept in detail, and make a case on its relevancy to the business and HR worlds.

Law Enforcement Concept #1
Situational Awareness

The primary concept and probably the most fundamental operating principle for law enforcement is a term known as situational awareness.

Every cop I know uses the term but, more importantly, hopefully, also incorporates it into every minute of their day, on duty and off. Cops know that acts of violence can occur at any time, by any individual, and at any location. In my life in law enforcement, I have met hundreds of victims that stated, through tears streaming down their face or blood running from some wound, "I was only going to get a gallon of milk" or "All I wanted to do was bring my clothes to the dry cleaners," or a million other variations that relay their surprise by being victimized at a place, at a time, or by a person that was not expected. These victims were all caught off-guard. In short, they were not situationally aware. I recently typed the words situational awareness into the YouTube search bar and it brought me to one video that made me laugh and worry simultaneously. The video is funny and eye-opening. It is about certain people who go through life in a bubble, pay no attention to the world, and the potential dangers all around them. The video is short and when it begins, the viewer clearly understands that he/she is watching a camera that has been installed on someone's porch. As the video opens, you see quite a large bear slowly walking on all fours on a suburban front porch. Suddenly, the bear stops and his attention goes towards the front door.

The bear is situationally aware.

Nature has equipped him to be aware. The viewer quickly realizes that the bear has stopped because the front door is opening. Out pops the first human from the house onto the porch. That person is an elderly woman, followed shortly thereafter by an elderly man. The woman enters the porch, and never looks right and never looks left. She never sees the bear. The husband exits the house and he too never grasps that they are mere feet away from a potential killer. The video concludes as the elderly couple exit the porch while the bear sits there still. Those two elderly people have never read this book. I'd love to send them a copy. That is if the bear didn't get to them first.

We can't afford to be that situationally unaware in the work environment. Especially as leaders of the organization and/or as HR professionals. I looked up the definition of situational awareness (SA) in several different sources and the major points of all these definitions included variations of the following statement: being aware or conscious of your surroundings (or environment) in an effort to identify or locate any/all potential threats to you or the environment. The most obvious example I can provide, that will illustrate the overall concept of SA, is flying on a commercial flight. When the doors close, but before the plane starts to leave the gate, the airline employees begin a process to make you situationally aware. The airline gives you an overview of the environment and the potential dangers you could face during your flight. They discuss turbulence and show you how to counteract its negative consequences by correctly using your seat belt. Even on flights between Kansas City and Des Moines, they alert you to the location of life jackets (in the unlikely event of an emergency water landing). They literally tell you the number of emergency exits on the plane as well as point them out to you. They go into further detail with anyone seated near an exit row. They discuss emergency lighting and that green lights will lead to red lights blah, blah, blah. The odds of you experiencing anything other than the occasional bout of turbulence is quite rare. So, why do airlines do this? Well, FAA rules of course, but what they are doing is providing you with situational awareness. They are pointing out the dangers that you might encounter, providing you with knowledge for surviving these dangers, and thereby hopefully saving your life.

Let me ask you this, how many people on the plane, that was so artfully landed on the Hudson River by Captain Sully Sullenberger, wished they had spent a little more time listening to those instructions when it very quickly started hitting the fan shortly after takeoff? While on the subject of flying and situational awareness, because of my current job and my experience as a Secret Service agent traveling almost on a daily basis, I routinely instruct senior leaders on traveling safely for business. One of the things I discuss with these seasoned travelers is the

"Plus 3, Minus 8 Rule." I became acquainted with this rule after hearing about a book entitled *The Survivors Club*[2]. In short, the rule encapsulates the fact that many experts advise that the most dangerous parts of any flight occur during the first three minutes after departure, and the last eight minutes of the flight. So, how does that information help the people I instruct? Simple. 'Forewarned is Forearmed.'

Specifically, be awake, be aware, and be prepared as the flight departs. Know where those exits are and know which one is your first option and which one is the second. Keep your shoes on and don't take a nap during the takeoff and upon descent. Who is more situationally aware and prepared to survive, the person following this rule or the hundreds of passengers you have witnessed sleeping upon takeoff, with eyeshades on, noise-canceling headphones over their ears, shoes, and socks off, and wearing one of those squishy pillows around their neck? I will bet on the rule follower every time. There is a person that I would categorize as the father of situational awareness, and that is Colonel Jeff Cooper of the U.S. Marine Corps. He is a legend on this subject matter and his brainchild, named the "Cooper Color Codes" is the bible of situational awareness. It has been embraced by the military and the folks in law enforcement. I would argue that managers and HR representatives need to do the same. Cooper

---

2 Sherwood, Ben. *The Survivors Club: The Secrets and Science That Could Save Your Life.* New York City: Grand Central Publishing, 2009.

created the color-coding system many years ago, and it has stood the test of time. It is a simple theory and it is hard to argue against. Cooper wanted to express, in visual terms, the fact that Marines needed to be situationally aware in order to survive, especially in battle. So, Cooper came up with a very easy to understand and easy to teach theory that combined a color graphic with an associated color-coded chart. There were four colors to the chart and associated with each color was a state of awareness and preparedness. I personally know of no one in the military or in law enforcement that has ever argued with the theory, and I have literally heard it discussed in training sessions at least fifty times in my career. With credit and admiration to Colonel Cooper, he argued that Marines can operate from one of these four states. I will encapsulate his idea, and explain the four states below.

- White: You are not situationally aware at all. You are unaware of your surroundings. Picture the two elderly people in the bear video.

- Yellow: You do have situational awareness but you are still relaxed and calm. You are not easily surprised while operating in this condition. Picture a proactive security officer making his rounds.

- Orange: Something in your environment has increased your attention and awareness. Something is amiss. You need to address it so you begin planning and evaluating the situation. Picture that same security officer making his rounds and observing an idling car in the parking lot and an open window to the business.

- Red: The bad thing is happening. You are now placed into action (fight, flight, or freeze). Picture the security officer being confronted by someone exiting the open window with a crowbar and a laptop/computer in his hand.

I don't believe that in Cooper's original thesis there was a fifth color, but I have been seeing more and more of these SA charts also displaying the color black.

- Black: You panic, you completely lose any control over the situation.

I would make the case that leaders in the business world and HR representatives can't afford to operate in condition white very often. In fact, as I wrote this section, I wracked my brain and tried to come up with a scenario where it would be ok to operate in condition white in the workplace. If you are responsible for people's lives or their careers, there really is never a good time to operate in condition white. The one scenario I came up with was this: It is after hours, or on the weekend, and you go into work to catch up on administrative functions. The weather is clear, and there are no other employees in the business. The security officers are patrolling the grounds and, like the old Christmas poem, not a creature was stirring, not even a mouse. I can understand that one might find themselves very readily in condition white and probably rightfully so.

In December 2015 in San Bernardino, CA, a group of employees got together at an event center to participate in an office Christmas party. There was food, drinks, and people were enjoying themselves. The employees were experiencing the goodwill and fellowship that comes with the holidays. There were toasts, laughter, and photos around a Christmas tree. If there was ever a better place for condition white to exist, I can't fathom one. Although I was not there, I have listened to some of the survivors tell their story, and I can deduce that most of them were operating in condition white and I would have expected nothing less. And then the gunshots rang out. Rizwan Farook and his wife Tashfeen Malik, two fellow employees who had trained in terrorism tactics overseas, took that exact moment to unleash hell on their colleagues. At the end of that event, there were fourteen fatalities and twenty-two people were seriously injured. The offenders were also killed in a long-running gun battle with the police.

The problem with operating in condition white is the fact that when that bad thing happens, the person in condition white gets thrown immediately, and with no warning, into another color code. The worst scenario that can be imagined is going from condition white directly to condition black. Many times, that ends up with the person dead. That is why it seems that cops and soldiers never seem to let their guard down a hundred percent. They maintain some level of alertness and continue to scan the environment for potential trouble. It can be done without appearing like a nut and can be accomplished subtly. I don't know how many of those folks at the Christmas party were in condition yellow but I would guess some were. I wonder if it helped them. You have all heard the old adage about cops always eating in restaurants with their backs to the wall and in a place where they can look at the entrance/exit. It is *not* an old wives' tale, and it shouldn't be. It is the truth, at least that is what every training officer attempts to inculcate in new officers. Why would cops do this? They have experienced the randomness of violence and know how quickly it can start and how quickly it can subside. They are looking to give themselves every possible advantage which includes knowing the surroundings and looking for baselines and anomalies (more about that later), adding to the chances of survival.

In November 2009, Maurice Clemmons walked into a coffee shop in Lakewood, WA, and with no apparent warning, shot four police officers while they sat in the restaurant. I have no idea which Cooper color those officers were in seconds before the shooting, but I know that in the blink of an eye, they found themselves in another Cooper color entirely. That exact type of incident is why cops think like they do, act like they do, and sit where they do. That adage about cops sitting with their backs to walls is situational awareness in a nutshell. Cops want to know where possible threats to their safety might come from. So, if they sit at a table with their backs to a wall, now they only have to worry about threats from the front and sides. With that simple placement, they have increased their safety exponentially. If that seat also places them in a position to watch the entrance and exit, they can spot a threat in the parking lot before it enters the building.

If you take situational awareness to the extreme, the officers would also look for a table as opposed to a booth, because it is easier to escape from a table than a booth. Really smart officers also drive through the parking lot and around the back of the restaurant first, looking for possible concerns. They park away from the front door, backing into the parking space so they can leave quickly if they had to pursue someone or drive a victim to a hospital. They take their time walking in. They walk in slowly and are using all of their senses. They are listening for issues (yelling, noises), they are watching for issues, and they are using their sense of smell. As they enter the restaurant, they scan the entire building from top to bottom and right to left. They are looking for anything out of place. They are looking for problems and they are hoping that they see none. Although I never served in the military, I have personally witnessed veterans and SWAT team members shudder when they find themselves in a setting surrounded by higher ground. In their subconscious, the part of the brain where situational awareness lives and breathes, they know inherently that the person who has the high ground in any battle has an extreme tactical advantage and that the person(s) below are at an extreme disadvantage.

I know what you are thinking! You are probably thinking that you coordinate the benefits section of an HR department or you run a corporation or you lead a group of engineers or factory workers or you run a chain of restaurants, why would you want to continually operate in condition yellow? You are perhaps saying to yourself that operating in condition yellow, under ordinary circumstances, is not normal, it is probably paranoia, and it is being overly reactive.

"Why would anyone want to operate like this in real life?" I hear you.

The answer to that question is simply beautiful. When cops walk into a restaurant, they take in all of the information, they scan people and the environment and they look for baselines and anomalies, all the time acting normally and not acting oddly or strangely. It is as normal a behavior as walking or talking. Because it is now part of their everyday lives, it literally takes no extra energy from their end. Simply put, they have embraced, no, they have incorporated, situational awareness as a way of life. It is part of their brain's hard wiring. It is a survival skill that is as normal and involuntary as breathing in and out.

A great thing about operating in condition yellow is that it doesn't feel any different from condition white. All you are doing is looking a little closer at things, playing the "what-if" game in your head, and going about your business. In short, you are just a little more engaged and you have skin in the game.

Situational awareness is an easy practice to latch onto and to improve upon. A great way to start practicing this behavior is to 'people watch.' The next time you find yourself in a public place, pull up a bench, chair, or stool, and start the process. As you scan the crowd, look for baselines and anomalies. Look for people or things that seem out of place or whose behavior differs from the rest. Watch people as they interact with others. Create stories in your mind about who these people are, what they do for a living, are they married or single? Try to determine if anyone you are watching might actually be carrying a weapon, legally or illegally. It is an interesting way to pass time especially with a significant other. But it also sharpens your observational skills and makes it easier to incorporate these skills in environments that might be unsafe.

Business leaders and HR employees know that workplace violence, or other workplace emergencies, like medical conditions or weather-related incidents, can occur without warning at the job site. The affected employees will be looking to you for guidance and support during the incident. Why on earth would you not want to practice situational awareness in the workplace, embrace the concept, and make it create a safer environment for yourself and your team? It is literally the least you can do, based on your position, to help those that you are responsible for. One caveat about the subject of situational awareness that you should always remember is that we are not asking you to be paranoid. There are no boogeymen or ninja behind every door. We are merely asking you to be aware, be awake, and be curious. Dr. Kevin Gilmartin, an expert on police stress, has written books and articles on what he terms "hypervigilance," that is when cops become too paranoid about potential dangers in their work environment. Gilmartin discusses the physical and emotional toll on cops who remain "on-guard" too much. We are not asking you to be hypervigilant, but only engaged. After all, you are of no help to yourself or your charges if you see a threat everywhere you look. Your workplace is almost always a safe environment, but we are asking you to be aware of signs and clues which tell you that something is amiss.

Law Enforcement Concept #2
Command Presence

I hate to say it, but people still do judge books by their cover. Every day the people that you work with in your organization make assumptions about you and your leadership skills based on your appearance and your demeanor. I am going to make the case for dressing like a professional and acting like a professional in the workplace. Cops have a term for it, they call it "command presence." All officers are taught the concept of command presence on their first day at the academy. I have also heard it being called 'military bearing.'

Today's work environment often dictates a relaxed dress code and an informal style of interpersonal interaction. In fact, when I was the security director for a multi-billion-dollar corporation, the CEO would ask me to call him by his first name. I couldn't do it. In my view, he would lose some of his command presence if I called him by his first name. Fire Chief Ron Richards, on a website designed for emergency service personnel, wrote an article about command presence. He defines command presence as 'the act of presenting yourself as someone in authority, someone who is trusted and respected.' He says that command presence is the overall impression have over others by how you look, how you carry yourself, how you act, and how you speak. Richards argues that first impressions are lasting ones. In addition to giving the impression that you know what you are doing, he writes that dressing professionally actually makes you feel more confident.

He then offers advice on how to improve command presence through body language, the way you speak, and the way people see you (Richard 2004).

So, why would an HR professional or a business leader want to display command presence? The answer is obvious. Our employees and others we come in contact with are evaluating us just like we evaluate them. If they perceive those in HR or leadership as true professionals, they are less inclined to test us or, literally and figuratively, fight us. People want to be led by and advised by professionals. In reality, we owe it to these people to be professional in all that we do. Looking, acting, and dressing the part is one of the easiest ways to professionally interact with people. If Fred from Accounting has an

issue and decides that he is going to seek a redress of grievances, or is looking to seek advice, shouldn't he be met by
someone who takes his/her appearance and position seriously
and respectfully?

Let me show you how important command presence has
been historically in the field of law enforcement. A few years
back, the U.S. Supreme Court changed how courts would
look at officers who used force during an incident. In short,
the court came up with the 'Reasonable Officer standard'
to judge whether an officer used proper or excessive force.
The court asked all juries and judges to evaluate an officer's
use of force against the proverbial average reasonable officer. The court stated that these evaluations should be made
using only the information known to that officer at the time of
using force. For example, an officer gets an anonymous call
that a man, short in stature, is standing outside a convenience
store and the caller saw what he thought was a handgun in
that person's jacket pocket. The officer arrives at the store and
the person flees on foot. The officer chases the person, and as
the person rounds a corner, he removes the handgun from the
coat pocket and turns towards the officer. The officer fires his
weapon and shoots and kills the suspect.

During the subsequent investigation, it is determined that the
"short male" was actually a tall fourteen-year-old boy and the
gun in question was actually a toy replica. The courts would
ask the agency, the judge, and the jury to review the officer's

actions based on what the officer knew at the time of the shooting. Would a reasonable officer react in the same way given the same set of circumstances?

But before that Supreme Court decision, almost every agency in America had what was called a 'use of force continuum.' It was displayed visually in various ways by different departments, but almost every agency used an 'if-then' type of diagram. 'If' the violent individual used this type of resistance or violence 'then' the officer was allowed to use this type of force. It was very confusing even in a classroom setting and was even more confusing for officers dealing with a resistant or violent offender in real life. Cops were forced to make split-second decisions while trying to remember what the color-coded and confusing pyramid said about the situation.

Why do I spend so much time telling you about the use of force policies in law enforcement? Because before the Supreme Court made the decision-making process easier and more practical, almost every agency in America started their 'use of force continuum' with the words 'command presence.' Almost every law enforcement agency in America showed that an officer's mere presence, in uniform or via his/her comportment, was by its very nature a way to control people. So, just by showing up and looking authoritative, every agency felt that officers could impact people and make them do what was required by law. In essence, just by displaying 'command presence,' police officers can gain compliance and cooperation from people.

As an HR professional or an organizational leader, don't you want to gain cooperation and compliance from folks? The easiest way to do that is to start on the right foot and show command presence by always dressing professionally and acting appropriately. So, by dressing like a professional and acting like a professional you are having a psychological impact on the people within your organization. You need to harness that and use it for good. Exude competence and confidence, and you can create a safer work environment.

In the Secret Service, we referred to people who looked or acted unprofessionally as 'soup-sandwiches.' I have never heard that term anywhere else but in the Secret Service and, initially, it didn't make much sense to me. But in your mind's eye, try to picture what a soup sandwich might look like and you come away with an image of something that, on its face, can't look very good. You never wanted anyone in the agency to refer to you as a 'soup-sandwich.' Someone with command presence would never be called a 'soup-sandwich.'

Bad guys and troublesome employees attempt to defeat 'soup-sandwiches.'

In my role as an instructor at FLETC, I have had the opportunity to listen to the recorded interviews of numerous prisoners who were incarcerated for life or who sit on death row for killing police officers. During those recordings, I heard many prisoners admit that they looked at responding officers and mentally evaluated those officers. The prisoners never used the term 'command presence' but many of them talked about making a decision on the officer's skill set based on the officer's appearance. I remember one prisoner's interview distinctly. Speaking about one of the officers he assaulted, the prisoner stated that the officer's uniform had wrinkles in it, his shoes were not polished, and he was not authoritative in his demeanor. The prisoner said in the interview that he took one look at him and judged the officer to be out of shape, not highly trained, and easily defeat able. That officer lacked command presence, and because of this deficiency, he unknowingly invited the criminal element to test him.

Do not ask to be tested in the workplace. Be approachable, be friendly, but also always have a command presence. Who knows how many potential problems you will avoid because of your confidence and your professionalism thwarted it in the infancy stage? So, if your company allows jeans or shorts in the workplace, I would argue that a pair of khakis and a nice company branded polo shirt will immediately make you appear more authoritative and professional. If your company dress code is slacks and a polo, wear a shirt and tie. In the Secret Service, we were always taught that we never wanted to be underdressed in any environment. Always better to be over-dressed than underdressed.

Law Enforcement Concept #3
Cover and Concealment

When I went through three different law enforcement academies, as a field training officer and as a law enforcement instructor, the most-simple concept that came up again and again was the concept of cover and concealment. How simple are these concepts? This is how I have explained the concept to hundreds of young law enforcement officers, and to every employee I meet during the 'active-shooter' portion of new hire orientation.

Cover is any object that can stop or seriously slow down a bullet's trajectory.

Concealment is any object that hides you from a potential threat.

Cops and military veterans are always subconsciously looking for cover and concealment in their surroundings. Of course, they prefer to find cover and not just concealment, but something is better than nothing.

The first time I put cover and concealment into practice and didn't just see it as some ethereal and nebulous concept, was when I was a young police officer. I can assure you that I had never before searched for cover more than on that day. It started when I was dispatched to a fight in progress. No big deal, right? In my short time in the police department, I had been dispatched to a hundred fights in progress. The address of the fight seemed innocuous enough, a fast-food restaurant at a fairly large intersection inside the city. Oh yeah, I forgot to tell you that the call I was dispatched to occurred on a night when two rival inner-city high schools met for their annual football game, and this restaurant was just blocks away from the neutral football stadium. As I pulled into the McDonalds parking lot, there were at least two hundred people in the restaurant and parking lot, each person wearing the colors of one of the two opposing football teams. There was screaming, punching, kicking, and just general mayhem going on. As I arrived as the first cop to this mini-riot, I exited my patrol car. As I searched the crowd to see where and how I could start to restore order and protect any innocent parties, I observed a male, about twenty-five yards from me, take up a shooter's stance. As my attention became fixated on him, I saw this man raise a handgun towards me, and then, simultaneously, I saw a muzzle flash and heard the sound of gunfire. There were dozens of innocent people behind the shooter so there was no way for me to return gunfire. It was exactly at that time, that I wanted cover but would be willing to settle for concealment.

Early in my career, I chose not to wear my bullet-proof vest but instead chose to carry my vest in my trunk. As they say, youth is wasted on the young. I was a college graduate but I wasn't very smart. At that moment, I knew I wanted that vest on and I wanted to put it on from behind cover. I was able to make my way to the trunk, place the vest over my uniform, and take up a position from behind the cover and concealment of my rear fender, wheels, and tires. I never did find that shooter but I wore my vest every day after that.

As a business leader, you should not have to learn the very important lesson of how important cover and concealment can be in your workplace survival mindset, in the same stupid way that I did. The need for cover and concealment can happen anywhere, at any time. I want to direct you to a video that will reinforce that declaration. They say a picture is worth a thousand words, and I agree wholeheartedly. The video I want you to watch will visually show you the concepts of cover and concealment and will explain it better in a matter of seconds than I ever could in twenty pages.

Go to your favorite search engine and search for one of the following terms.

- Lawyer dodges bullets
- William Striler shoots Gerry Curry

But do me a favor, don't search for the generic terms like "Client shoots attorney," because you will find all sorts of stories and videos that clearly illustrate the breadth and width of workplace violence.

If you find the video I am trying to show you, it will bring you to a one or two-minute video of a shooting on October 31st, 2003 at the Van Nuys, CA courthouse.

Feel free to put this book down and watch the video. I will wait here, while you watch it.

Welcome back!

The video captured a client attempting to shoot and, I would imagine, kill the attorney. The scene takes place outside of a courthouse, and the shooter unleashes all the rounds in a revolver towards the attorney. The attorney, who I can only guess was probably already in condition yellow based on the subject's previous actions, reacts amazingly under the circumstances. I have no idea if the attorney in the video knew the difference between cover and concealment but he exercised the concepts perfectly, probably saving his own life in the process. The only thing between the attorney and the client, at the time of the shooting, was a tree.

A small tree.

A very small tree.

A Charlie Brown Christmas type of tree.

But any port in a storm. The attorney did exactly what he should have done. With few options available to him, and facing a crazed client pulling out a gun and shooting at him from close range, he used cover, concealment, and movement. Oh yeah, one last thing. The distance between the attorney and client could be better measured in inches as opposed to feet.

The attorney Gerry Curry, used that little sapling as concealment and as cover. In addition, the attorney used movement
to his advantage. I can't do the episode justice in writing, but
that video shows in real-time how movement, concealment,
and cover can vastly increase your chances of survival.

As Secret Service agents, we would routinely go to refresher
training at our training facility in suburban Maryland. One of
the many courses we were exposed to were ambush attacks
on us while protecting a government leader. During many of
these training scenarios, both the students and the instructors
were armed with paintball guns. Anytime we had scenarios
take place on the cover and concealment range, I knew I
was going home with some lessons learned, and a couple of
bruises (on my body and psyche) as well. I distinctly remember
during one of the training scenarios, I was ambushed by an
instructor, and literally, the only object I could move towards,
that provided any cover or concealment, was a fire hydrant.
Now, I am not a tall guy... but a fire hydrant? Come on man!

I tried to make myself as small as I could even as paintballs
started flying my direction, as I simultaneously tried to shrink
behind the hydrant and return fire, the instructor took advantage of any part of my body that was exposed. The first thing I
left dangling outside the hydrant was my left elbow. POW! The
instructor found it with a paintball pretty easily. I brought that
body part in, now stinging from the paintball and oozing red
paint. Still trying to make myself as small as I could, I let my knee

extend past the hydrant. POW! Now the knee was blue and reeling from the sting. It is amazing how small you can make your body when you need to.

So, why do I think business leaders and HR types need to know about cover and concealment? It is like knowing how to change a tire or drive a stick-shift, you may never need that knowledge but you will feel more comfortable knowing that you can. How much more confident would you feel in the workplace, especially as a leader, if you knew where to go and what to look for in the event of an emergency. Leaders are supposed to have some baseline knowledge in many subjects, knowing how to use cover and concealment might just enable you to protect your subordinates from danger.

Law Enforcement Concept #4
Position of Advantage/Disadvantage

In law enforcement, during any potential violent arrest or other dangerous scenario, officers are taught to place themselves in a position of advantage and place the potentially violent offender in a position of disadvantage. Let me give you an example. An officer has an arrest warrant for someone who is known to be armed and violent. The officer locates the individual driving his car down a city street. So, to create a position of advantage, the initial officers seek out additional officers to assist him/her. Then the officer looks for the most advantageous location to stop the individual. The officers initiated the traffic stop and took up a position of advantage behind his vehicle (using cover and concealment). The offender is ordered to assume a position that allows for the offender to be at a physical disadvantage and the officers are thereby placed in a position of advantage. That is why during an arrest, an offender might be ordered to lay on the ground on his stomach with his arms and legs extended wide. Or, the subject might be ordered onto his knees, crossing his ankles, with his arms extended over his head. In short, the officers want to have a tactical advantage, (physically, mentally, and psychologically) over the potentially violent individual.

But how do you incorporate this dominating and highly tactical concept in today's politically correct and highly sensitive workplace? Easy. It is done subtly, with prior planning, and it creates a safer environment but no one is even aware it is being incorporated. Here's an example:

Let me discuss one of my pet peeves as it relates to the position of advantage in the workplace. I have seen dozens of managers and HR representatives place themselves in a position of disadvantage during counseling or termination sessions. That has to stop now, and hopefully, this chapter starts that process. First of all, we all need to admit that there is a fair amount of psychology that already exists in the workplace and that as managers, we need to control that psychology and use it to our best tactical advantage or else the potentially violent colleague will use it to his/her advantage. With that in mind, let's discuss the concepts of the position of advantage/disadvantage during an employee counseling session, suspension, or termination.

First of all, the primary and most important factor in determining the location of these types of meetings with employees is safety. The safety and security of the managers involved, the safety and security of all other employees, and the safety of the employee being counseled, suspended or terminated. Secondly, we as managers or HR professionals decide where and when the meeting takes place. We are in control, and therefore it is we who decide the timing, the location, and the physical set-up of the meeting. Do not let the tail wag the dog in these types of meetings. If the timing isn't correct, or if it is an unsafe environment, then the meeting is delayed or postponed until the conditions are right. In exigent circumstances we still want to make the site the safest it can be, with the cards we are dealt.

So, what are some of the factors that go into deciding where this type of personnel action can take place? This is not an exhaustive list but some suggestions about where the location should be:

- Close to the exterior door of a building.
- Close to security (or close to a place where security can be staged).
- In a private and neutral setting.

- Away from distractions.

- A place that is not likely to cause further embarrassment to the affected employee.

- Not psychologically empowering for the affected employee (like his or her office).

- Physically barren environment, i.e., devoid of any item that could potentially be improvised into a weapon. Yes, that means no pictures on the wall unless they are bolted to the wall. No pens, pencils, scissors, other office supplies in the room. No table lamps etc.

Once the location has been selected, it is imperative that the leader ensure that they, and not the disciplined employee, have the position of advantage. What do I mean by this? Here are some examples of establishing a position of advantage for the business or HR leader.

- First of all, the employee should not be allowed to bring in any extraneous items into the room. Psychologically, the employee is given strength by bringing in items with them. Your concern should be for physical safety so no bags, briefcases, etc. should be allowed in the room. As a polygraph examiner, I occasionally had subjects bring items with them to the exam room. They knew they intended to lie to me and they wanted to psychologically gain strength from that item. On several instances, I had examinees bring bibles, photo albums, or other very personal items with them. On each occasion, I asked them to leave those items outside the room. Those items are distractions and do not belong in that type of meeting.

- All writing instruments can potentially be used as weapons so they should be few in number, and controlled by the leader.

- The leader should always invite the employee into the room and instruct/guide the employee where to sit. The leader, and not the employee, should control the environment. We should be sending a subconscious message that management is in control of the environment.

- The placement of people at the desk or table is imperative. The use of the concepts of time, distance and barriers, cover and concealment, and movement are paramount here. Specifically, the employee should be placed well inside the room with their back to the wall, farthest away from the exit door. The leaders, on the other hand, need to be closest to the exit door. If the employee decides to become violent, the leader will use the proximity to the exit door to escape. Having a table or desk between the leader and the employee provides for what Gavin DeBecker calls the "moment of recognition," the time it takes you to realize that there is a threat and the time it takes to act on it.

The room should have some type of communication device. So, if the meeting goes South or there is some violence, there is some way for the leader to summon assistance. This type of communication tool could be a panic button, a phone, a handheld radio, or maybe the ability to have a closed-circuit television monitoring the room (without recorded audio of course).

If a manager goes into one of these scenarios and is not aware that there is a psychological thriller going on, he or she should not be in their current role. I spent a good portion of my career conducting interviews and interrogations of people in matters small and matters big. I can assure you that to the person being interviewed, interrogated, counseled, or terminated, there is a huge mental chess game being played. They are looking to defeat you or at least win you over. They intend to keep their job, blame their performance on others, or to convince you that the action you seek to take is wrong or unjust. They will do what they can to psychologically beat you. If you don't realize that you have already lost.

To ignore that fact is to put yourself and your other charges in danger. In the capacity of a polygraph examiner, I interrogated people every day. I can assure you that everything that I, (or any other Secret Service polygraph examiner), did in that interview room was done on purpose. Everything was done to subtly and non-violently establish psychological dominance, build rapport, and promote safety, or to lower the inhibitions of the person being interviewed. Nothing was left to chance and nothing was done haphazardly. What was the result of these actions? Like all other Secret Service polygraph examiners, I maintained a confession rate in the mid-nineties range. That meant that if I evaluated someone as being deceptive during a polygraph exam, I would interview or interrogate them. The result of that interview process? About ninety-five percent of the time, the subject confessed to the matter at hand.

I know what you are thinking. You are a manager in the private sector or an HR representative, you want to be a partner to the employee and you don't want to psychologically defeat them. You are not a cop, and you don't want to be; you want to help your company and your co-workers in being productive.

I could not agree with you more!

The beautiful thing about the concepts we discuss in this book is the fact that these concepts can be deployed and no one will ever notice them. Very simply put, you are just seeing things through a different lens now. You can still be friendly, you can still be professional, but now you will just be thinking proactively about safety and security concerns. You, as a leader, can establish dominance, build rapport, and create a safe environ-ment and do it in a very unassuming and professional way. As I said, I was very good at obtaining confessions from guilty peo-ple. It is a learned skill. Hundreds and thousands of investigators have the same skill-set. But I obtained all of those confessions without ever once raising my voice, without ever once being rude or unprofessional. Well, that is not entirely true. There was one time when I was interviewing a pretty hardened criminal, and no matter what I did, he would not confess. I spent hours with him, trying every tool in my toolbox to let him bare his soul to me and acknowledge the truth. It was only then that I tried to play the verbal bad cop. It did not go well. Within seconds of me changing from the good cop, he invoked his constitutional rights and left the exam room.

I cannot begin to tell you the number of times I obtained a confession from someone, a confession that would stand up in court and more than likely cause a finding of guilt at trial. A confession that would make him/her spend lengthy sentences in prison, and at the end of many of those confessions, the subject would thank me and shake my hand. You can create a safe work environment and still control the physical environment. You can still be seen as a partner and a friend, and ensure that you are following the tenets laid out in this book.

As a police officer, I gave out many more warnings on traffic stops than I did citations, but in almost all instances, I controlled the actions of the citizens on those stops. Like thousands of other cops, on a daily basis, I was able to be professional, friendly, but also in control. I used a low-key approach, a calming voice, and a body language commensurate with what I was trying to say. Again, I was always amazed at the fact that in those instances, when I did write a traffic citation, the driver, more often than not, shook my hand and thanked me at the conclusion of our interaction. Like chewing gum and walking simultaneously, it is possible to be seen as friendly, approachable, and professional, while at the same time making sure that you are putting yourself, and the people or company you represent, in the safest position you can. You, as a leader, can establish your position of advantage in these types of personnel actions without ever looking mean or overbearing. You can do it without violating policy or industry standards. It just starts with a different mindset. A mindset that you will create a safe workplace, and that you won't allow a problem employee to use their emotions or intelligence to defeat you in performing your role as caretaker of the workforce.

In personnel actions, just like in criminal interviews and interrogations, the affected employee is operating from a script where he/she will do whatever it takes to maintain their job, their position, their benefits, or their reputation. All of their actions are being perpetrated to achieve their desired goals. Having an employee choose to sit in a seat nearest to the exit door and forcing the manager or leader to sit in a far corner is not done haphazardly. Either consciously or subconsciously, the employee chose that specific seat. It is part of that chess game. You need to control the chessboard from here on.

Law Enforcement Concept #5
Pre-Assault Indicators

When I was an instructor at the Federal Law Enforcement Training Center, I was one of the dozens of veteran cops whose duty it was to train the next generation of professional law enforcement officers. In addition to ensuring that the newest generation maintained high standards of ethics and physical fitness, we always wanted to make sure that the trainees remained safe in this dangerous profession. We strived to impart in the students, hints and tools of the trade, to ensure their safety. There was no concept more basic and more important than the concept of pre-assault indicators, and we reinforced this concept by showing the trainees countless videos of real-world attacks on cops because they needed to see it on video so that they recognized it in real life. In a nutshell, the concept of pre-assault indicators states that human beings will almost always telegraph the fact that violence is about to occur. It is a tell, just like a bad poker player will have a tell if he has a hot hand.

Sometimes these pre-assault indicators are verbal and sometimes they are physical in nature. I have watched so many dash-cam or body-cam videos of cops getting assaulted that it used to make me nauseous. I used to get mad and frustrated at the cops in the videos because with each pre-assault indicator being displayed by the perpetrator, I felt that we, as trainers, had let those officers down. We had not prepared them well enough to watch for or listen for those behaviors or statements that predict an impending assault. Many of the videos we showed only resulted in bruising the egos of the cops. Some ended in injuries to the officers and some resulted in tragic deaths of American heroes.

HR representatives and business leaders routinely interact with people in the workplace who could become violent. As a leader, you must know what to look for, and be prepared to disengage and/or de-escalate the situation. When I explain in further detail, some of the verbal and non-verbal cues that predict violent behavior, I want you to think about the actions of the employee I discussed in the first chapter, who while his managers were seated, stood up, took a bladed body position, raised his hands, gestured wildly at his managers and yelled, "You're yellow and you're yellow." In my mind, and the mind of most people attuned to human behavior, all of those actions were pre-assault indicators and should have been treated by the HR manager as such. If my former employer truly had a zero-tolerance policy against workplace violence, that type of behavior would not be tolerated.

So, what do some of these pre-assault indicators look like or sound like? Some of the cues given by soon to be violent people are very subtle, while some are not. One of the videos, that I remember distinctively showing the trainees, was of a subject who just kept repeating the same phrase to the soon to be assaulted cop. That statement? "Man, I can't go back to prison." It came out as "Man, I can't go back to prison," but what he was actually saying was "I am not going to allow you to take my freedom away," or, " I am going to do whatever it takes, including killing you, to keep from going back to prison."

There was another video that we used all the time to reinforce the concept of pre-assault indicators, and this one video was instrumental in training new officers because the offender gives at least a dozen clues that he planned on becoming violent. From memory, the subject makes some verbal admissions that are indicators of future violence and the subject also takes off his hat and places it on the hood of a car, the subject then rolls up his sleeves, removes his watch, and performs a series of other 'grooming' behavior.

Taken all together, the soon to be attacker was telegraphing in multiple ways that violence was about to take place. Shame on any business leader or HR employee who is exposed to these pre-assault indicators and doesn't recognize them for what they are. One of my fellow instructors, a good old boy from the South, would stop the video at important parts and reinforce to the trainees what they were seeing. When the subject took off his hat and placed it on the hood of the car, this instructor would ask the students, "Is this normal behavior? Why would a man take off his hat?" The instructor would laugh and explain to the students that where he came from, a man only takes off his hat for two reasons, one of the reasons was to have sex and the other was to fight. Either way, the instructor would jokingly say, it was not going to end well for the cop in the video.

To better illustrate some of the specific actions that make up pre-assault indicators, I searched for a comprehensive article that I felt was a one-stop shop for learning more about this subject matter. A search on the internet found exactly what I was searching for. The article was written by Greg Ellifritz and appeared on the website of 'Active Response Training.' The article is entitled "How *to Spot a Bad Guy- A Comprehensive Look at Body Language and Pre-Assault Indicators"* [3]

I wholeheartedly endorse Ellifritz's article in its entirety and I would beg you to read it, understand it, and incorporate his writing into your daily work routine. Out of respect for Ellifritz, I will not cut and paste his statements here, but I will hit the high points of his writings:

- Pre-assault indicators are universal. Ellifritz states that they appear in all cultures and any environment.

- He asks you to be alert when you see "predatory move-ment patterns."

- He asks you to pay close attention to the hands, lower body, arm movements, and respiration of the subject.

- He cautions about seeing the "thousand-yard stare" in someone's face.

---

3   https://www.activeresponsetraining.net/how-to-spot-a-bad-guy-a-comprehensive-look-at-body-language-and-pre-assault-indicators.

- He discusses the psychology behind physical actions of the subject to "hide" their intent such as masking behaviors and grooming cues.
- He details "target glancing" and the act of "looking around."

As a manager or HR personnel, you should have a baseline knowledge of pre-assault indicators and Ellifritz's article is a great starting point. It will make you and your employees safer, but more importantly, it will provide you new insight into what constitutes workplace violence.

Law Enforcement Concept #5A
Always Watch the Hands

I couldn't pass up the chance to discuss what every cop in the world knows. You always have to watch the hands. It is the hands of the criminal that causes the assault or the injury. Cops are always scanning their entire environment (see situational awareness above) but the one area that they concentrate on the most is a person's hands. It is the hand that holds the gun or the knife. It is the hand that makes the fist. It is the hand that, during that termination, will hurt you. It is the hand. It is always the hand. As a manager, business leader, or HR professional, you need to always watch the hands.

Law Enforcement Concept #6
Baselines and Anomalies

I can't introduce the concept of baselines and anomalies without thinking about that old Sesame Street song entitled "One Thing is Not Like the Other." That song was used by the Sesame Street characters on numerous occasions to teach kids to differentiate between things that are alike and things that are different. There is probably no technique that has caught more criminals and thwarted more attacks than the fact that the offender or potential attacker acts "differently" than the non-threatening people.

Cops and threat assessors are taught to look for the baseline in locations and situations, and then to be alert for behavior that is incongruent to that established behavior, also known as an anomaly.

As a Secret Service agent in training, I was instructed to look for baseline and anomalies. One of the real life scenarios where this theory was readily apparent were the actions of John Hinckley while he made his way into that makeshift press pen, outside the Washington Hilton, before the Reagan assassination attempt. In hindsight, you can clearly see that he did not "fit in" with the surrounding crowd. I have reviewed the still photography of the terrorists that killed their co-workers during the San Bernardino Christmas party. Their behaviors were definitely not baseline in nature. Let me be clear, baselines and anomalies have absolutely nothing to do with profiling people based on age, race, sex, religion, or any other type of classification that is discriminatory. In short, it is about monitoring people, crowds, or some other population, discerning how that group acts as a baseline and then looking for anyone acting outside the norm. It is about actions, behaviors, non-verbal cues, and so on.

Phil Carlson, a former career cop, law enforcement trainer, and current security director often make presentations to large civic groups on various topics. In his presentations about active shooters, he often discusses looking for baselines and anomalies. To make the subject matter easy for understanding, he asks his audience members to provide him with the baseline behavior of people attending a religious service. Depending on the makeup of his audience, he may get the following responses as baseline behaviors:

- Well-dressed
- Quiet
- Reverent
- Solemn
- Slow-moving
- Ritualistic behavior
- Singing
- Praying
- Smiling
- Crying

At this point, my friend will take a minute and jokingly discuss that the attendees of a typical Southern Baptist Church service will have vastly different baseline behavior than the attendees of a Roman Catholic service in urban Philadelphia. Then, my friend asks his audience to describe the baseline behavior of the average NFL fan in any given stadium on a Sunday evening game. The list usually looks something like this:

- Excited

- Energized

- Vocal/Loud

- Animated

- Dressed in the team's uniform jersey and/or team hat

- Drunk or slightly inebriated

- Constantly in motion (sitting, standing, cheering, waving arms)

Then my friend makes the comparison that elucidates the difference between baselines and anomalies. To parishioners attending a religious service, the behaviors listed in the baseline description are all normal. What if an NFL fan stormed the church, temple, or mosque, dressed and acting like the person described in the second list? What if a devoted parishioner appeared at an NFL game, dressed in a suit and tie, and sat quietly with his hands folded in prayer? Those would clearly be anomalies from the baseline behavior of the more general population.

This baseline and anomaly behavior became quite clear to me as a young man when I was working my way through college as a store loss prevention officer. I spent my days watching people in the store as they went about their business. People who are not intent on stealing anything act with a certain baseline behavior. It is fairly easy to observe someone in this environment and make a determination almost instantly that they are just baseline shoppers.

On the other hand, it is also fairly easy to look at someone, and due to their actions and their attempts to conceal their intentions, determine that they plan on shoplifting. Most baseline shoppers are paying very little attention to what is going on around them but thieves are always looking around, attempting to act nonchalant, as they search for loss prevention officers, witnesses, or closed-circuit television cameras. These anomalies were behaviors that I saw in people of both sexes, of every race and religion, and had absolutely nothing to do with profiling. It was their actions that caught my eye, not the color of their skin or their genetic makeup. I held that job for two years, and I can only think of one person who displayed anomalistic behavior and didn't steal; I can't think of any one individual who did steal that did not display non-baseline behavior first. Of course, that is all anecdotal evidence but there is science behind this concept as well.

You, as a leader or HR professional, need to know what the baseline actions of your employees are and be on the lookout for anomalies. Those anomalies might just be pre-cursors to violent actions.

Law Enforcement Concept #7
Reactionary Gap

In short, the reactionary gap refers to the space that cops maintain between themselves and others. It is more than just the personal space that we all maintain as a cultural norm; it is a survival instinct. All cops know that actions are quicker than reactions, so every good police officer attempts to leave a little more distance between themselves and the people they interact with. Of course, this is done without creating so much distance that the officer looks foolish or can't verbally interact with people effectively. It is just a little bit of extra space, which allows the officer a minuscule amount of additional time to "react" to a threat. So, it is a gap that officers attempt to maintain between themselves and potentially violent people. Of course, this gap is relative and increases or decreases in size based on the circumstances. If cops are dealing with a lost child, an elderly woman, or some other seemingly innocent situation the reactionary gap closes. But if they come in contact with a potentially volatile situation or person, the reactionary gap tends to get larger.

Business leaders and HR representatives should keep the reactionary gap in mind when dealing with employees in highly-charged environments. Leave a little distance between yourself and the employee being terminated or counseled. Even better, keep an obstacle (barrier) between yourself and them, as well as increase your distance. Of course, use common sense and don't be so far away that you look ridiculous, but just keep a little extra distance between yourself and the potential problem. That extra amount of space might just bide you enough time to protect yourself.

Law Enforcement Concept #8
De-Escalation and Face-Saving Techniques

After thirty years in law enforcement, I can declare that the difference between a good cop and a bad cop is the ability to read people, empathize with people, and speak to people. I have worked with cops who could calm down the most aggravated people and I have, unfortunately, worked with cops who made every situation worse with their lack of interpersonal skills. As a cop or an agent, I loved going to calls or investigations with the former and hate interacting with the latter. I have never run away from a fight and I have had to go "hands-on" with more people than I want to remember, but I can assure you that, if given the option, I would much rather talk to a person than fight with them.

The secret to convincing them to act non-violently is the ability to engage in de-escalating and face-saving behavior. There are dozens of books on de-escalation and face-saving techniques. There are countless websites devoted to the subject, and there is a cottage industry of consultants and trainers that instruct on employing de-escalation techniques in both the public sector and the private sector. Like I just said, there are dozens, if not hundreds, of organizations out there that claim to teach HR leaders and business folks how to de-escalate in the workplace. But, continuing in the vein that law enforcers and threat assessors have a unique perspective and skill set in this subject, I want to recommend that the readers of this book take one specific course on de-escalation. Some of the best training I have seen in this subject comes from a retired police chief who now runs his own consulting group, the Dolan Consulting Group. This former chief, Harry P. Dolan, offers several types of de-escalation courses for cops and emergency medical personnel. One of the courses offered is called "Verbal De-Escalation Training: Surviving Verbal Conflict." He offers one of these classes online. Although it is targeted specifically for police officers, the course is relevant for anyone who deals with human beings. Especially human beings in the workplace that might be going through some type of crisis. The course is about seven hours in length and, at the time I am writing this, the cost of the course is ninety-nine dollars. In my opinion, the class would be a bargain at five times that cost.

In this online course, Chief Dolan uses common sense, and even some Aristotle, to teach you about how to de-escalate potentially troublesome interactions. Chief Dolan says that you can de-escalate people by appealing to what Aristotle called their 'ethos, pathos, and logos.' In other words, you can make an ethical appeal, an emotional appeal, or a logical appeal.

The link to the online course is https://survivingverbalconflict.com/

I recommend this course without any reservation if you are an HR employee or if you lead people in any organization.[4]

Some people are born with de-escalating skills and some aren't. But this is a talent that can be learned.

I won't pretend to make you a de-escalation subject matter experts in this short chapter, but I will make a few suggestions. First, you can't go wrong by always employing the golden rule of treating people like you would like to be treated. Secondly, lose the ego. In order to de-escalate any situation, you have to be selfless. You have to be calm yourself as well.

Location is to real estate, like empathy to de-escalation. It is probably the most fundamental tool in the de-escalation tool kit. It is the duct tape of de-escalation. You can use it in every circumstance. Remember that I said empathy and not sympathy. The online dictionary defines sympathy as 'the feeling or expression of feelings of pity or sorrow for someone else's misfortune.' The same dictionary defines empathy as 'the ability to understand and share the feelings of another.'

---

4 Disclaimer: I don't know Chief Dolan, have never met him, and don't receive any remuneration for recommending his training, but I have taken the training myself and I am a believer. In addition, he and his firm enjoy a stellar reputation over the subject matter

In de-escalation incidents, the enraged or offended person does not want your sympathy, but they will appreciate your empathy. Your ability to empathize with an aggrieved person, to walk in their shoes, or to see the incident through their eyes, will make the de-escalation process much easier. They don't want you to feel sorry for them, they want you to feel what they are feeling and to validate those feelings. You don't have to agree with their feelings but you should understand what they are feeling and why they are feeling it. In addition to using empathy, you will want to employ a steady, calm, and low voice and demeanor. You can't respond to being insulted and you must let negative words and statements act like the water off of the back of the proverbial duck. You have to make yourself and the surrounding environment appear as non-threatening as possible. Now, this might sound oxymoronic but you have to act self-assured, and in control of yourself, without looking cocky or being pretentious. You have to display that command presence we discussed earlier. Don't stare the folks down and use appropriate eye contact for the situation. Don't point at them and keep a socially acceptable distance from them. Do something to "connect" with the other person. Find some common ground. See if they will engage you on a personal level. If possible, try to use their name while speaking to them if you can incorporate it naturally. Employ active listening techniques. Try not to interrupt them while they are speaking. Acknowledge what they are feeling and don't pass judgments on those feelings. You don't have to agree with what they are saying, but at least acknowledge their feelings. Repeat back what the person is saying, and ask for clarification. For example, "So, Fred, I hear what you are saying, and just so I understand better, I heard you say that your boss is playing favorites with your co-workers and you are being made to work the overnight shifts because she likes the others better. Is that what you are saying? Do I have that correct?" When possible, ask the escalated person to offer up their solutions or ways to find common ground. Common ground is very important. If possible, try to get the person to agree with you about part of the issue. If you can get them to say yes, you have already started forging a bond and have started the de-escalation process. When appropriate, try to get the subject to begin discussing future plans and take him/her away from what is currently the issue. Try to instill a sense of hope and promise into the scenario. Introduce optimism into the issue at hand. Don't make promises you know you can't or won't keep. Be truthful to the escalated individual and never lie to them. If you can't agree to what they are asking, explain to them your reasoning and once again seek common ground. Attempt to make the escalated individual feel valued and explain to them that his/her opinion is worthy of your time. Never rush them or make them feel that they are not important. I would be a rich man if I had a dollar for every time some agitated person was able to calm down after simply allowing me to hear their side of the story. I literally have had at least a hundred agitated people say to me, "all I wanted was for someone to listen to me." You need to be that sounding board.

Whenever I come in contact with an agitated person, I literally start following a script in my mind. As a law enforcer and security director, I have been placed in too many situations where I was forced to interact with an aggrieved and agitated person. The script always begins in the same way, if I don't know the person, I attempt to introduce myself by name and my role, and by understanding how I can help them. Something like this, "Hi, my name is Kevin and I am in charge of the security function here at XYZ, and I was told that you might need some assistance. Do you have a minute to speak with me? I'd like to help you if I can, and if I can't help you, I will try to find someone who can?" For me, that style of approach has worked wonders over the course of thirty years. More often than not, this type of initial approach has started the process of de-escalation. You need to find your script and make it work for yourself. In the course offered by Chief Dolan, he calls this first step of the de-escalation process the "meet and greet."

If you are interested in digging deeper into the subject of de-escalation, I think there is no better starting point than Chief Dolan's online class. It is meant for public safety officials, but its relevance is universal in any workplace. Oh yeah, one last piece of advice about de-escalation. When terminating someone, don't ever say anything like, "This is what you get when you make poor life choices."

Law Enforcement Concept #9
The Power of 'What-If' Scenarios

As you lead people in business or the HR field, you are coming in contact with people during their highs and their lows. They spend as much time with you under that roof as they do with their loved ones. Of course, there are going to be arguments, mindless turf battles, office romances gone sour, and the obligatory disciplinary actions, suspensions, and terminations. Any time you get people together for long periods of time, especially under trying conditions, there will always be the potential for violence. I hope that you, as a leader, are playing the "what-if" scenarios in your head before, during, and after any significant personnel action.

What do I mean by what-if scenarios?

My friend and colleague Phil Carlson tells young cops, and his business audience members, about the Cooper Color Scale we discussed previously. He says that the brain is like a computer and when a stressful, dangerous, or violent incident occurs, the brain immediately starts searching for a file detailing this type of event and how to solve it. Phil tells his listeners that if the brain has been (hopefully) trained for this type of scenario before, the brain finds that file and acts on it. If the brain searches and searches for that file and finds nothing, the fear is that the person goes straight to "black" on the color scale, and either panics or does nothing to solve the problem. The result of panicking or doing nothing in an incident like this in the workplace can be damage to property, poor public relations, or in the worst-case scenario the death of employees.

Let me give you an example, we have all sorts of files that our brain maintains for emergency situations. When we were small, we were trained that if we ever caught ourselves on fire, we would 'stop, drop, and roll' until we extinguished the flames. I, fortunately, have never caught myself on fire or been near someone who has, but I am pretty sure my brain has been hardwired to respond with those three-word set of actions if I ever do. Even though I knew about 'stop, drop and roll,' I think back to when I was about six years old. It was winter and we lived in upstate New York, everyone in the family wanted to ice skate on our frozen pond. Before my parents were comfortable enough to let everyone on the ice, my Dad said he had to check it first. To this day, I don't know why he did this, but my Dad brought me to the pond, sat me on the dock, and then started walking the ice-covered pond. My dad told me that if he fell in, I should run back home and get help. I can tell you that at six years of age if my Dad fell in the water, I was prob-ably going to panic and be of little use. At that tender age, I had not played the 'what-if' game before. What if Dad falls in? Do I throw him that rope, do I stay here, or do I go get help? There was no file for that subject matter in my young brain.

Every year since I graduated high school, I have held a job where I had to get certified on, among a dozen other subject matters, the use of a fire extinguisher. That may sound silly, but you might be surprised to know how many people in this world have not been exposed to operating a fire extinguisher. Learning how to use a fire extinguisher is not something you want when you realize that your kitchen is on fire, or your neighbor's car is engulfed in flames. If there is no file in the hard drive (your brain) for extinguishing a fire, the fear is that you are either going to be useless or, at least, waste very valuable time. So, once a year, you will find me and many others in my chosen career fields, sitting behind a monitor for an hour, taking a computer-based learning module detailing the different types of fire extinguishers and the types of fires that they will extinguish. You will hear the narrator discuss the PASS method of extinguishing a fire.

In case you are unaware of that particular acronym, let's create a file of our own today. 'PASS' stands for the four steps of using a fire extinguisher.

> P: Pull the pin
>
> A: Aim the nozzle at the base of the fire
>
> S: Squeeze the handle to activate the extinguisher
>
> S: Sweep the extinguisher back and forth

Because my brain has this 'PASS' file in its memory bank, I am one hundred percent confident that I will be able to effectively use a fire extinguisher in case of a fire. By creating 'what-if' scenarios in our head, we are creating that computer file in our brain. It is potentially life-saving in nature.

My partner and I, when I was in the police department, would engage in dozens of 'what-if' conjectures. We created and role played, in thoughts and actions, our expected responses to imaginary circumstances. For example, we imagined and played "what-if" scenarios for being held at gunpoint, to being held hostages, and dozens of other possible scenarios. We played out scenes like "what if a bad guy gets one of our guns from us?" We talked that scenario through in a million ways and we came to agree that if one of us was disarmed and the bad guy ordered the other to surrender his weapon, that we would not comply with his demand. My partner and I came away from that particular 'what-if' game knowing that if one of us became disarmed, the other would not acquiesce and would violently end the incident. He and I also discussed being taken hostage, and both of us agreed that we would never allow one of us to be taken from the scene by a bad guy. Because we worked through dozens of these 'what-if' scenarios, we had created code words for each other so that we could convey information to each other without other people know- ing what we were talking about. We had a sentence that we would speak to each other which would mean nothing to the by-standers, but to us, it meant that we had probable cause to arrest an individual and we had to act quickly because we feared he/she would be violent if we did not act quickly.

If you are a business leader or an HR professional, you and your co-workers need to occasionally sit down together and brainstorm some 'what-if' scenarios. Here's one to start with. "What will we do if someone (let's say Fred from Accounting) ever barged into HR and started getting loud and threatening, but does not attack anyone yet?" Or how about this: "What should the administrative staff do if someone calls the C-Suite and threatens the CEO?" You need to create those computer files in your collective brains now before it's too late. It will build confidence in your team and it will also show them that you are proactive and care about their safety.

Law Enforcement Concept #10
Signs of Weapon Carriage

In the first chapter of this book, we laid out some statistics about the numbers and types of violent acts that can occur in the workplace. Luckily, per capita, these types of incidents are fairly rare and we are not trying to convey to you that you work in a dangerous place. We are not trying to make you paranoid. But, let me ask you some simple questions that go to the heart of human nature in the workplace. Do you think an employee you lead or represent as an HR representative has stolen from the corporation this week?

Do you think an employee you lead or serve has lied in his/her role this week?

Do you think an employee has cheated the corporation this week?

Do you think an employee in your group is disgruntled?

Do you think any of your employees have been violent to a spouse, child, or co-worker this week?

If you are being honest, depending on where you work, you probably said yes to some or many of those questions. With that in mind, I want you to answer the following question:

Do you think one of your employees has brought a weapon to work this week?

If you said no to that question, in my humble opinion, based on my training and experience, I would say that you are either naïve, wrong, or both. Even though almost every company has rules against bringing weapons to work, many employees still possess them in the workplace. It's not always guns, but many bring knives, chemical weapons like pepper spray, extendible batons, and a myriad of other weapons. Some do it because they fear an active shooter situation, some bring it to feel safer walking to and from their cars in the parking lot. Some do it because they fear a co-worker. Some have exes or stalkers that they worry about visiting them in the workplace. No matter the reason, my experience has shown me that many employees are armed in the workplace. Couple that with the fact that every study on mass attacks and workplace violence has shown that firearm is the weapon of choice for these types of attacks. With that fresh in our mind, we thought it would be best to devote some time to this book on the subject of concealed weapons. Specifically, we wanted to educate leaders and HR representatives on how to best spot someone who is attempting to conceal a weapon, especially a firearm. Law enforcement officers visibly scan every person they come in contact with, and they are searching for any telltale sign that the person might be carrying a weapon.

The first thing we need to discuss is the fact that weapons, especially firearms, are heavy (usually) and are very difficult to conceal easily. Having said that, there is an art and science to concealing a weapon so that it is not easily discovered. There is a cottage industry of weapons manufacturers, holster makers, clothing lines, and accessory companies all trying to offer products that better conceal firearms. In addition, there are hundreds of writers out there, in print and on the internet, discussing better ways to carry and conceal firearms.

In my experience as a gun-toter for thirty years, both on duty and off duty, I have learned that carrying a concealed weapon is always a fight between three competing interests:

- Easy access

- Weapon security

- Concealability

Pick two, because trying to accomplish all three is a rare feat.

The easier it is to access, the more noticeable it generally is. Many times, the manufacturer of the latest and greatest concealed carry holster system promises better concealability and easy access, but the weapon is not very secure. I have bought at least a dozen products and have spent hundreds, if not thousands, of dollars in my career on products that all promised a high degree of concealability, weapon security, and easy access. And, I have yet to find a product that offers me all three; so when you try to carry a concealed firearm, you are always sacrificing one of the three to satisfy the other two. In my case, I am very comfortable with my solution. My personal solution provides weapon security and a high degree of concealability, but I sacrifice a little bit of speed of access. In thirty years of carrying concealed firearms, I have only had one person identify that I was carrying a weapon.

Having said all that, for the safety of you as a leader, for the safety of your employees, and for the safety of the employee carrying concealed weapons, you should know what to look for when it comes to weapon concealment.

Once again, without being paranoid or irrational, you as a leader in business should be able to subtly scan problematic employees or employees involved in troublesome situations, and look for the readily identifiable traits of concealed weapon carriage. Keep in mind that carrying a firearm, especially in the workplace, is not acceptable behavior and these employees are attempting to hide a heavy, large metal object; so many times the weapons are kept in their car or in their locker. If you don't have a screening process at your workplace, they may store the weapon in their purse, backpack, or briefcase. Some may even keep it in a locked drawer at their desk.

Guns are, by their very nature and due to their size and weight, hard to conceal. Many people will attempt to conceal it anywhere but their own body. But if they decide to actually carry the weapon on their person, you should look for the following signs:

- Security checks: People carrying concealed will often "check" their weapon. They fear that the weapon might fall out of the holster, or might get seen, so they are always confirming that the weapon is secure. This is usually done by feeling for the weapon/holster with their hands or elbow. If wearing an ankle holster, they will often check their pant legs with their other foot.

- Printing/Imprinting: People carrying a weapon are always in fear that the outline of the gun or holster will appear on their clothes, so they often wear clothes that are loose, baggy or ill-fitting, to avoid the imprinting of a gun on the clothes.

- Unnatural Gait: A person carrying a gun moves differently from someone who is not. Learn to look for the differences.

- Sagging pockets: Some weapons are so small that they are designed to be carried in the front pockets of pants. Even if they are the smallest of weapons, it still causes pockets to bulge or sag. Look for those signs.

- Bulges: Are you seeing bulges where there shouldn't be any? The most obvious places for weapons carriage are the hips, the small of the back, the front waistband, and the ankles. But there are a dozen products out there designed to cleverly conceal a weapon in places not usually suspected, like in the cleavage area in a bra.

- Strong side away from people: People carrying a gun will oftentimes attempt to move the side of their body with the gun, away from other people, so that they don't brush up against someone who could feel the weapon. Look for those strange body movements.

- Clothing styles don't match: Is it hot outside and the person is wearing a jacket, vest, or two shirts. Is everyone else wearing shorts but one person is wearing long pants, and he seems to have a bulge around his ankles?

- Rigid arms/arm movements: Once again, trying to conceal the existence of the gun by concealing it with his/her arm.

Not every employee is carrying a weapon, but learn to start looking for any/all signs of weapons carriage. It might just save your life and the life of those you work with.

Law Enforcement Concept #11
The Attack Cycle

I don't want to spend too much time on this concept because you are not a soldier, and you are not a cop. But I wanted to at least introduce you to the concept of the attack cycle, sometimes called the 'terrorist attack cycle.' Because violence, especially violence that is found in the workplace, is often pre-mediated or planned, I want to explain the concept. Before almost every attack in history, there is an attack cycle that takes place.

In bullet form (pardon the pun), the cycle goes something like this:

- Initial target selection
- Surveillance of target(s)
- Final target selection
- Pre-attack surveillance
- Planning
- Rehearsal
- Execution (Attack)
- Escape and exploitation (If not suicide attack)

So, why should you as a business leader or HR representative know the attack cycle?

You should have a baseline knowledge of what the cycle looks like for some very obvious reasons. You need to know what it looks like so that, in case it is happening, you have some grounding in terms of what is happening. Let's say some customer, Fred from Cincinnati, bought your product and it sickened his child. Let's say Fred has a bone to pick with you and he feels the need to get even. Wouldn't it be nice to know that if Fred is going to travel to your city to seek revenge, he would probably engage in this attack cycle? The goal would, hopefully, be to identify his behavior during the earlier stages of the cycle and not later. Wouldn't it be great if your security team approached you and told you that they just stopped a guy in the parking lot, a guy named Fred from Cincinnati, who was taking pictures of the parking lot and employee entrance? Knowing what the attack cycle is, provides you with more intelligence about the best way to respond to Fred from Cincinnati. Or say you discover that a former terminated and disgruntled employee (say Fred from Accounting) was seen across the street from your CEO's house, and when the cops stopped him, he had a stun gun, rope, and duct tape in the car. Now that might mean your former employee took his wife's car to the hardware store to pick up some home improvement items, or it might be part of an attack cycle. But you need to know what the attack cycle is, in order to make better decisions about the safety of your employees and your organization.

Law Enforcement Concept #12
WIN: What's Important Now?

Organizational leaders and HR personnel are constantly being pulled in different directions, with their priorities always changing. Many times, it is hard to follow a North Star and keep on track. That is never more the case than when some type of crisis or perceived crisis visits your organization. Don't you wish that there was some simple rule to follow in that crisis? Something easy to follow, that didn't require a flow chart? Something that buys you time? Something that ensures you always do the right thing first and prioritize everything else as well.

Well, there is a concept so beautiful in its simplicity that I believe all leaders should know it and follow it. The concept is especially powerful and impactful when a leader needs direction during a time of crisis, or when the organization or their employees' lives are at stake. The concept did not originate from the law enforcement or threat management fields but comes to us from a college football coach. Yes, a college football coach! Not just any coach, but coaching legend Lou Holtz. He called his approach, WIN, for 'What's Important Now?'

Holtz's WIN concept was later adopted by law enforcement, and it has caused a different mindset in that profession and has changed lives and saved lives. I personally have adopted the concept in my daily life, especially during times of crisis when it keeps me on track. Many times, the concept has kept my ego intact and has informed my decisions in a very practical way. The concept is as deep as it is simple, as sweeping as it is focused, and it is universal in its application. I personally heard about the concept for the first time while attending an annual conference of the International Law Enforcement Educators and Trainers Association (ILEETA), which was being held in a convention center just outside of Chicago. I had been scheduled to make two presentations to that assembled group on a very different subject matter. A matter that, I felt, was negatively impacting the law enforcement community, and my goal was to provide some common-sense recommendations to the attendees about how to improve our chosen profession. But, when I heard a presenter speak on the WIN concept, it blew me away and made my presentation pale in comparison. Luckily, the law enforcement profession, mainly through the work of one man, has adopted the concept in order to improve itself. I would urge leaders in HR and the private sector to do the same.

The presenter (and main proponent) of WIN, or 'What's Important Now,' was Brian Willis, an institution in police training circles. Willis is a retired Sergeant with the Calgary, Canada Police Service, and is the Deputy Executive Director of ILEETA. Willis is now the president of 'Winning Mind Training.' I would highly recommend you check out his website at www.winningmindtraining.com

As Willis spoke to the assembled group of hundreds of police trainers from around North America, he held our collective attention, and as any police trainer will tell you, cops are a tough audience. Cops, as a general category, especially as an audience, are Type-A personalities. They are judgmental and they are always sizing up the presenter, with their BS detectors on the high setting. But Willis held that audience in the palm of his hands. No small feat. That accomplishment was due to his presentation skills but also because of the concept itself. It is such a simple concept, one could argue that it is intuitive in every human being and doesn't need to be mentioned. Except, it does.

In his presentation, Willis immediately acknowledged the original author of the WIN concept and gave credit to Lou Holtz, the legendary former head coach for the University of Notre Dame. Willis spoke about how Holtz had written about WIN in a book, and how Willis had heard Holtz speak on the subject as well. Willis outlined how the coach used the WIN concept on his football team and how the utilization of WIN as a mindset and a roadmap ultimately led to a national football championship for Holtz and Notre Dame. After giving due respect to the coach for originating the concept, Willis began speaking about how we as cops, and especially as teachers of cops and as leaders in the law enforcement field, could incorporate WIN into our professional lives. The WIN principle, Willis stated, would not only make us safer and more productive but would also make those we serve and protect, safer. As I listened to Willis talk, I could immediately see the applicability of the WIN concept in my own managerial decision making. I could see its universal appeal to any cop on the street trying to make split-second decisions, and living with the consequences of those decisions. More importantly, I saw that this concept, as written and spoken about by Holtz, a concept about creating a National Champion on the gridiron, has immediate and relevant application to leaders in the HR and business worlds. Well, that is too limited, the concept is applicable to any human being who finds themselves making choices that impact the lives of others.

But, before we go further into how law enforcement adapted the WIN concept, let's take a look at the concept itself, as Holtz created it. The concept appears in the coach's book *Winning Every Day*. Holtz's book, at least the edition I have, is two hundred and nineteen pages in length and is chock full of sage advice from one of the winningest coaches in all of sports history. Coach Holtz is known as a motivator with common sense approaches to leadership. In this book, which is filled with inspiration on numerous subjects, Holtz's discussion of the WIN concept appears in only three paragraphs. It almost seems like an afterthought that Holtz even mentions it. Coach Holtz introduces the WIN concept by detailing a personal near-death experience, where he was thrown off of a white-water raft. Holtz suggests that people use the WIN approach so that "they won't waste time on the trivial" (Holtz 1998, 107). A few pages later, Holtz brings up the WIN concept for the second and last time in the book. The coach discusses coaching one of his very successful college football teams and states: "Building a successful team is easy. Just bring together a group of people who dream of doing the impossible and have them follow the WIN formula" (Holtz 1998, 112).

In his presentation, Willis recalls seeing an interview of Holtz where the coach spoke about how WIN worked with his football team. According to Willis, Holtz asked his team if they wanted to be the national champion. To their obvious reply, he then told them to ask themselves what's important now, a hundred times a day. It would look something like this:

As a student-athlete, looking to be a national champion, you should ask yourself what's important now? The first answer of the athlete should be "I need a good night's sleep." Upon waking up, the students ask WIN and the answer is "I need to eat a nourishing and healthy breakfast." The next WIN response is "I need to work out," the next WIN answer is "I need to go to class," and so on. What gets excluded from these types of WIN questions if you are seeking to become a national champion? The use of drugs, alcohol, criminal acts, etc. As Holtz described in the book, the trivial goes away and only the important things remain.

To me, it is amazing that a couple of paragraphs in a two-hundred-page book could make such a positive impact on law enforcement as a profession. Lou Holtz wrote the book for anyone interested in winning and leadership, but law enforcement took the concept and expanded on it. That field took the definition of what it means to WIN and made it applicable to public safety.

What does winning look like in law enforcement? And how does the WIN concept get utilized?

In law enforcement, wise decision-making, and simple guide-posts that are capable of being used in exigent circumstances, are godsends. So, getting your average cop to ask themselves 'what's important now,' a hundred times during a respective shift, can be a calming and reassuring navigational beacon for them. The concept of WIN allows an officer to leave his or her ego in check, and take a second to reflect and gain some perspective.

What do I mean by that? Because of the nature of the pro-fession, being placed in highly charged situations where the officer is expected to solve the problem at hand, oftentimes police officers allow emotion to get in the way of good deci-sion making. Sometimes, egos can get in the way of making the right decision. Let's take vehicle pursuits for example. In any given year, more police officers die in the line of duty, as a result of motor vehicle crashes, than by gunshots, knife attacks, or other physical injuries. That fact is borne out year after year. An average officer might initiate a traffic stop, and when the offender doesn't immediately stop, the officer's adrenaline goes up and he feels like his authority has been questioned. The officer doesn't usually know why the offender isn't stopping. Is it because his license is suspended or revoked? Is it because he is a wanted fugitive? Is it because he just robbed a store and killed the cashier? Sometimes, the offender is indeed running from some heinous criminal act. Many times, the offender is running away out of stupidity, fear, or something minor, like some drugs in the car or unpaid tickets. At the very second that the offender begins to flee, an officer needs to make a split-second decision, do I pursue or let them escape? The officer thinks: Based on everything I know right now, what is the best response?

At that moment, is there a better three-word question the officers can ask themselves than, "what's important now?" Some of the possible answers the officer should playback in his head after asking, what's important now, include:

- Is it more important to stop the driver and risk an accident?

- Is it more important to chase him and risk my death, the death of a pedestrian, the death of an innocent driver, or the death or serious injury of the offender?

- Is it more important for society, for me to let this driver escape rather than putting others at risk?

- Is it more important to let my ego and my need to capture the criminal element supersede all other considerations?

- Is it more important for me to attempt to capture this driver by chasing him or through good old-fashioned investigation later?

Without a simple mantra and an easy-to-follow roadmap for good decision making, the average officer can easily allow the adrenaline induced emotions to take precedence and engage in every pursuit that comes along. Incorporating the WIN concept, however, allows that same officer to take a breath and gain some highly needed perspective. What really is important right now? Stopping the offender at all costs or using proper judgment to guide your decision.

There will be times when the right decision is to pursue the offender, and there are times when the right decision is to let them go and lessen the danger to innocent people.

From experience, I have engaged in several dozen high-speed pursuits during my career. There have been few other occasions where I have felt more alive and more energized. The thrill and danger of the chase, traveling at speeds in excess of 120 mph, all the while calling in information on your radio, using your siren, and trying to drive two cars (at least mentally, the offenders and yours), all in the pursuit (pardon the pun) of justice is some heady stuff. It is multi-tasking at its peak. Of those high-speed pursuits in which I participated, I never had WIN to guide my actions. In hindsight, there were many pursuits that I should not have engaged in, and it is only through luck and good fortune that I never killed or injured anyone. I wish I had the WIN concept back then, because I know I would have called off at least half of the pursuits I experienced.

But WIN helps cops not just during pursuits, but in all aspects of their professional workdays. Some citizen calls an officer a name or hurls some other type of insult. With WIN, the officer can put this temporary affront into perspective and de-escalate the situation. When confronted with a highly volatile and corrosive situation, WIN allows the officer to prioritize what is important at that very moment and delay any/all other actions until each "most important" activity is handled in order. An officer can address the most important item and then ask themselves: 'Now that I handled that, what's important now?' And so on and so on. Let's say an officer gets dispatched to a house fire, presumably to direct traffic away from the fire hoses. In this scenario, let's assume that the officer arrives before the fire department does. Directing traffic is no longer what is important now. If the officer asks what's important now, the answer invariably is this: 'determine if there are victims inside the house.' The next WIN question is this: 'If there are victims, how do I rescue them?' If there are no victims inside, the next WIN question is this: 'Do I need to provide aid to any victims standing outside?' If that answer is no, the next WIN question might be this: 'Do I need to move the victims to a safer location?' That officer might ask a dozen WIN questions before he arrives at the reason for which he was originally dispatched there, which was to direct traffic around the fire hoses.

The concept of WIN became universally accepted and part of mainstream American law enforcement when a group called 'Below 100' incorporated WIN into its program, designed with a very lofty goal. That organization was created and exists today with the intent to reduce the number of on-duty deaths of police officers in the U.S. to under one hundred officers per year, a statistic that has not occurred since the 1940s. The website for 'Below 100' can be found at www.below100.org

Their vision as an organization, according to their website, is that they want to eliminate preventable line-of-duty police deaths and serious injuries, through compelling common-sense training, designed to focus on areas under an officer's control. The last part of that vision statement "under an officer's control," is paramount. Whether it's law enforcement, Human Resources, or some other type of organization you are running, asking WIN allows the leader to concentrate on what they have, the power to change and to concentrate on priorities.

In order to achieve their published goal of less than one hundred police deaths per year, the organization known as 'Below 100' listed the 5 things that every officer should do to reduce the potential of death. Those five rules are:

1. Wear your belt (Seatbelt)

2. Wear your vest (ballistic vest)

3. Watch your speed

4. WIN- What's Important Now

5. Remember- Complacency kills

'Below 100' has a cadre of instructors that travel the country, reinforcing the five simple tasks that officers can do to immediately increase their chances of surviving that profession. They are five very common-sense rules to abide by. The first and third rules take into account that more cops are killed in traffic crashes than by any other type of incident. The second rule concerns itself with being assaulted by a bad guy with a gun or knife. The last rule concerns itself with situational awareness in this dangerous profession, a concept that this book has already discussed. But it is that fourth rule (WIN) that is comprehensive in nature. It concerns itself with every minute of an officer's shift. What is the most important thing I should be addressing right now, at this very moment?

That fourth rule, if used properly, encompasses all the other rules. Because if an officer is practicing the WIN principle, as he/she gets in their patrol car and asks WIN, the answer should be to buckle my seat belt. As the officer is dressing for work and asks WIN, he/she should say, I need to portray a command presence and I should have all of my gear so that I can protect myself and others. As he/she drives that patrol car and asks WIN, he/she should reply, I need to slow down and drive safely so that I can keep myself and others from danger.

Asking WIN provides officers with that North Star we discussed earlier. A path to follow.

The concept of WIN is never more important than in a crisis where a leader is faced with so many demands and limited information at the time. Asking WIN allows you to immediately begin the prioritization process. That is why I think the business world and HR leaders should learn lessons from law enforcement's acceptance of this very fundamental principle and incorporate it into their daily lives. As an HR leader or a manager in the private sector, the WIN concept allows you to accomplish what Coach Holtz alluded to. Ignoring the trivial and concentrating on what's important.

The WIN concept was created by a leader in the sports world, but law enforcement saw its potential and adapted it for the public safety profession, I would urge the private sector to do the same. Coach Holtz's goal was to lead a national championship team. He used WIN with his players to do just that. Think of what you could achieve in your organization if you incorporated WIN into your workplace.

So, as I sit here and write this section, I find myself asking What's Important Now? Right now, my answer to that question is the fact that I need to convince the readers of this book to see the relevance and the efficacy of Holtz's and Willis' work, and to use WIN to be better and more productive. If I have accomplished that, I can now move onto other tasks.

Law Enforcement Concept #13
Crisis Management and the use of an Incident Command System

If there is one thing that my time in both the public and private sectors has taught me, it is the fact that I know very little about business. I personally don't have an entrepreneurial bone in my body. Another thing I know and have personally witnessed is the fact that many business and HR leaders are highly skilled in their respective fields but they don't know squat about managing a crisis. Many of the private sector leaders I have worked with have never heard of an incident management system, or how to use it effectively to address some major crisis.

Case in point, as I write this section, my employer has been dealing with a crisis that has widespread implications for the organization. I watched the immediate response by civilians to this incident and came away unimpressed. The civilians had developed no workable, organized plan to address the issue. But then, the organization put someone schooled in the ICS protocols in charge (not me, by the way), and suddenly there was a plan and everyone knew their role. Without the oversight of someone with ICS background, I believe there would have been chaos.

That is because, almost all leaders in public safety agencies, like police, fire, and emergency management agencies are all taught the basics, and often advanced, protocols of a system that provides a time-tested, universal, and efficient way to effectively deal with a crisis of large magnitude. That system is called the 'Incident Command System (ICS).'

The ICS in the public sector was born in the 1970s, improved in the 80s and 90s, and was made mandatory in the 2000s by a presidential directive. It is ubiquitous in the public sector. You could take the police or fire captain from a mid-size city in the Southwest, and drop him or her into some type of drastic public emergency in Miami or New York, and that outsider could effectively coordinate that emergency. That outsider, although arriving from an agency thousands of miles away, would be speaking the same language and following the same basic script. The ICS model has been used hundreds, if not thousands, of times. It has proven its effectiveness, its simplicity, and its applicability in crises big and small. But when I speak of the ICS model to leaders in the private sector, I usually get a quizzical look.

I have watched several private sector leaders get tasked with responding to an internal or external crisis, and it seemed that each time they were flying by the seat of their pants with regards to creating a team for addressing the crisis. I watched them assemble a team haphazardly, often time selecting their cronies to fill roles. I have seen them concentrate on 'only' portions of the emergency, like messaging only to avoid or ignore other parts of the crisis. Having private sector managers trained in the ICS model, and having corporations comfortable with the ICS system, would allow for the prompt stand-up of an effective crisis management team.

Let's take a look at the ICS model in greater detail. I want to acknowledge the website of a private company, called EMSI, which has a comprehensive account of the history of the ICS system. I encourage you to visit that website to fill in the blanks that I leave here. The link to that page is www.emsics.com/history-of-ics/

According to the EMSI website, the 'Incident Command System' was born during the 1970 fire season in Southern California, when a group of multiple fire agencies created FIRESCOPE. The goal of FIRESCOPE was to better address the vast number of fires by establishing:

- Multiagency Coordination System (MACS)
- Incident Command System (ICS)

This new way of doing business in handling crises was overseen by the U.S. Forest Service. Their goal in creating a new system was to remove confusion at the incident level and the 30,000-foot level. The goal was to coordinate and handle competing for resource demands (EMSI, 2020). According to EMSI, the system created by the Forest Service operated off of four fundamental principles to combat crises (EMSI 2020). Those four principles included:

- Commonality and uniformity between responding groups.

- The importance of timely and accurate information in crisis management.

- The creation of procedures that will integrate and support a regional coordination system.

- The incorporation of modern technologies to improve response performance.

As this new system slowly evolved, by 1974, the modern-day ICS organization had been created, meaning that the standard ICS organization chart came to be. The modern-day ICS program consists of an Incident Commander at the top of the chart with four units reporting to that commander. Those four organizational units, that report to the incident commander (all with their own sub-units), created back then, and still operational today are:

- Operations

- Planning

- Logistics

- Finance/Administration

Although the ICS idea was originally created to combat western wildfires, it was readily apparent that this system could be used as an all-risk, all-hazard system. Meaning that the ICS program can be used to manage a crisis or incident of any nature (EMSI 2020). In the 1980s, the ICS system began being adopted by fire agencies throughout the country and was being used by FEMA. In the 1990s, ICS reached another milestone when the U.S. Coast Guard embraced the ICS process. In fact, the Coast Guards are ICS experts and they are seen as the cream of the crop in ICS training and usage. ICS became a universal crisis management phenomenon after the events of September 11, 2001. After that horrific day, it became apparent that public safety agencies needed to all be operating off of the same game plan. As a result, it was important for the ICS model to become the national standard for responding to crises. The best business practice as it were. As a result, on February 28, 2003, President Bush issued Homeland Security Presidential Directive 5 (HSPD-5). That directive was designed to increase the ability of the United States to manage domestic crises by establishing a single and comprehensive incident management system. This system called the National Incident Management System (NIMS) would fall under the Department of Homeland Security generally, and the Federal Emergency Management Agency specifically.

Over the last decade, the ICS model has been adopted in other countries around the world. It is a tried and tested way to clearly establish roles in an emergency. I would encourage all HR and business leaders to take a look at the ICS in greater detail and see if having some type of ICS model in their organization could lessen the impact of a crisis, if and when that time comes. And, that time always comes. There are dozens of companies out there that will, for a cost, teach the ICS model to your private-sector enterprise. Before doing that, I would ask you to take a look at the FEMA website, specifically the National Incident Management (NIMS) homepage. On that webpage, the federal government states that they stand ready to teach the private sector, and other groups, the ins and outs of incident management. Private parties can sign up to take the initial ICS course online for free. Please see the federal government ICS website at https://training.fema.gov/emiweb/is/icsresource/ for additional information.

Law Enforcement Concept #14
Learn How to Stop the Bleeding

As a leader in an organization, you need to be aware of the potential dangers facing the people you lead. Whether it is an industrial accident, a weather-related emergency, or an active shooter incident, your employees can potentially face a life-threatening medical emergency in the workplace.

Almost every cop in America has on their person, or at least in their car, a bleed kit, equipped with a tourniquet and other supplies. So many lives can be saved, and have been saved, by stopping the bleeding of a victim. I had the honor to listen to a doctor who was part of a SWAT team that responded to one of the worst mass shootings in America. I listened to him say that almost every person who died in that event died from blood loss and not from the actual gunshot. If an event like that were to happen in your organization, I suggest you be prepared.

Hopefully, you have positioned AED's and first aid kits through-out your organization, and have trained some, if not all of your folks, in CPR and basic first aid. But, I would also ask you to look at this realistically and teach your folks about saving lives by learning how to stop blood loss.

After the truly tragic events at Sandy Hook in Connecticut, the American College of Surgeons met to learn from this event, and others made recommendations to save more lives in these types of attacks. The results from this group have become known as the 'Hartford Consensus.'

The following statements have been taken directly from the website of the Hartford Consensus page of the American College of Surgeons:

"Military experience has shown that the number one cause of preventable death in victims of penetrating trauma is hemorrhage. Tactical Combat Casualty Care (TCCC) programs, when implemented with strong leadership support, have produced dramatic reductions in preventable death. Recognizing that active shooter incidents can occur in any community, the Hartford Consensus encourages the use of existing emergency medical techniques and equipment, validated by over a decade of well-documented clinical evidence.

The Hartford Consensus recommends that an integrated active shooter response should include the critical actions contained in the acronym THREAT:

- *Threat suppression*

- *Hemorrhage control*

- *Rapid Extrication to safety*

- *Assessment by medical providers*

- *Transport to definitive care*

While some may view the addition of hemorrhage control skills as yet another training requirement in times of constrained financial resources, the concepts are simple, proven, and relatively inexpensive; many law enforcement agencies have already adopted them as best practices. Life-threatening bleeding from extremity wounds is best controlled initially through use of tourniquets, while internal bleeding resulting from penetrating wounds to the chest and trunk is best addressed through expeditious transport to a hospital setting. Optimal response to the active shooter includes identifying and teaching skill sets appropriate to each level of responder without regard to law enforcement or fire/rescue/EMS affiliation. THREAT incorporates the proven concepts of self-care and buddy-care." 5

So, what does that mean for you as an organizational leader? It means that your personnel should know how to treat someone who is bleeding profusely. At the very least, they should know how to treat themselves if they were ever severely injured and needed to provide self-care. Saving a life from blood loss is pretty simple. Bleeding can be stopped through a variety

---

5   https://bulletin.facs.org/2013/06/improving-survival-from-active-shooter-events/

of methods based on location and severity (direct pressure, elevation, packing the wound, tourniquet application, etc.). Learning those concepts is fairly straightforward and relatively easy to grasp, so the confidence it would give your personnel cannot be measured. You have now given them a skill-set that can help them in their own personal worlds and the workplace.

Some people might resist the training, seeing it as scary or threatening, and that's okay. Make the training available for volunteers only. But, can you envision if a third of your work-force learned how to respond to a major bleeding event? The lives that could be saved are immeasurable. Oftentimes this type of training creates workplace camaraderie, unity, *esprit de corps*, and a sense of purpose.

This type of training is available in communities from many sources, such as the local fire department, community college, and certain charitable groups, but I am most familiar with, an organization called Stop the Bleed. I would suggest you start your research on this topic by consulting them. Take a look at their website and the training they offer at https://www.stopthebleed.org/

One last piece of advice, no matter where you receive the training, ensure that your organization maintains a supply of bleeding control supplies, like tourniquets, at your facilities. Prepared, not paranoid!

Law Enforcement Concept #15
Learn How to Gather Intelligence

The best and most effective police agencies know how to gather information. They develop reliable sources and they are seen as approachable. Information in law enforcement is called intelligence because it sounds sexier. In law enforcement parlance, intelligence is high-speed, low-drag, while information is boring. Many times, the most complex of cases or the most difficult of law enforcement situations are solved as a result of putting together dozens of small pieces of fairly innocuous bits of information. Once the myriad pieces are sewn together, they make a fabric upon which strong decisions can be made.

Good managers and effective HR departments in the private sector should be no different. You should be seen as someone who can keep confidence (while abiding by any law about mandatory reporting and confidentiality). You shouldn't be seen as an organization that relies on snitches, but in an era where the phrase "If you see something, say something" is universal, you must be seen as the place to go to say something. Make sure you foster the reputation that information can be passed to you in a judgment-free zone. You will be surprised at how much information you will receive. Someone will, more than likely, tell you about how Fred in Accounting has been acting weird lately.

CHAPTER SIX

"WHAT THE FIELD OF THREAT ASSESSMENT CAN TEACH MANAGERS AND HR EMPLOYEES"

Threat Assessment Concept #1
Profile of an Attacker

I could make this the shortest portion of the book. I could write what I need to convey in one sentence or maybe two.

Here it goes:

There is no profile of an active shooter. Period. End of sentence.

Or, I could say this:

There is no known profile of someone who commits workplace violence.

Or, I might have said this:

There is no profile of an assassin. We need to look at behaviors and context, and not look for a profile.

We can look at historical data, and it can provide you with some background information on who past attackers have been, but it can't predict future behavior. But instead of leaving you, the business leader, with no helpful information, let's look at what we do know about people who commit targeted violence, especially workplace violence and mass attacks.

Threat Assessment Concept #2
Targeted Violence, Threat Assessment, and Threat Management

Dr. Mario Scalora at the University of Nebraska in Lincoln heads up a 'Targeted Violence Research Team.' He is a member of ATAP and is a subject matter expert on targeted violence. So, when I needed the best definition for these terms, I went on his team's website. There, he defines targeted violence as, "Violence that is goal-directed, predatory, and focused towards a specific individual(s) (e.g., stalking, terrorism, sexual assault). He defines threat assessment as the process of gathering information in an effort to estimate the threat of violence posed by a person or group of persons. Scalora further defines threat management as the strategies that can be taken to prevent violence and mitigate a threat. In contrast to the assessment of impulsive behavior, law enforcement and mental health practitioners addressing "targeted violence" address situations in which there is the assessment of risk posed to an identified (or identifiable) target by an identified (or identifiable) perpetrator" (Scalora, n.d.).

The FBI defines threat assessment as the "systematic, fact based method of investigation and examination that blends the collection and analysis of multiple sources of information with published research and practitioner experience, focusing on an individual's patterns of thinking and behavior to determine whether, and to what extent, a person of concern is moving toward an attack. A threat assessment is NOT a final product, but the beginning of the management process. It guides a course of action to mitigate a threat of potential violence" (U.S. Department of Justice 2017).

The U.S. Secret Service National Threat Assessment Center has been conducting some great research and writings on targeted violence. As you would expect from an agency that attempts to thwart violence against our nation's leaders, they have been a fountain of useful information in the field of threat assessment. In their work entitled, "Threat Assessment in Schools: A Guide to Managing Threatening Situations and Creating Safe School Climates," the USSS outlined that six principles form the foundation of the threat assessment process; those principles are:

1. Targeted violence is the result of an understandable and often discernable process of thinking and behavior.

2. Targeted violence stems from an interaction among the person, the situation, the setting, and the target.

3. An investigative, skeptical, inquisitive mindset is critical to successful threat assessment.

4. Effective threat assessment is based on facts rather than characteristics or traits.

5. An integrated systems approach should guide threat assessment inquiries and investigations.

6. The central question in a threat assessment inquiry is whether the subject poses a threat, not whether the subject made a threat.

   - (U.S. Secret Service, p. 29)

Threat Assessment Concept #3
Leakage

In my personal opinion, the most important threat assessment concept for organizational leaders and HR employees is the concept of leakage. Why is leakage important? Because the existence of leakage tells us that there is usually a warning before violence occurs. Simply put, leakage is the intentional or unintentional communication by a subject to another person, about their intent to commit a violent act by means of an attack. It is sometimes referred to as leakage-warning behavior. The concept of leakage was first documented in 2000 by Mary Ellen O'Toole Ph.D. and later she and J. Reid Meloy Ph.D. partnered to write a paper entitled *The Concept of Leakage in Threat Assessment.* I would recommend you take a look at the paper, it will open your eyes as to how leakage occurs and where your employee might "leak" information. The link to the paper is: http://drreidmeloy.com/wp-content/uploads/2015/12/2011_theconceptofleakage.pdf

Leakage is the real-world example of Ben Franklin's old adage about three people being able to keep a secret as long as two of them are dead. It is hard for people to plan an attack, and not accidentally or intentionally secrete some portions of the plan to a third party. It is almost a universal truth. After almost every mass attack, law enforcement learns that someone knew of the attack or parts of the violent plan. Most of these people knew that the attacker had displayed concerning behaviors.

Knowing that leakage exists and that it occurs before almost every attack, is helpful to us as managers. The next time someone from Accounting comes to us and advises us that Fred in Accounting keeps talking about getting even with James in Purchasing, we need to listen a little closer.

Threat Assessment Concept #4
Pathway to Violence

The field of threat assessment has uncovered that violence, especially violence in the workplace, is not usually a sudden and unplanned action. Instead, what study after study has shown us, is the fact that targeted violence is well thought out and executed as the last part of a cycle. Statistically speaking, an act of violence in the workplace, or other public places, is a result of about two weeks of planning. This cycle, known as the 'Pathway to Violence' has several steps, and was documented by two giants in the threat assessment field, Frederick Calhoun and Stephen Weston. It is important to know these steps, and hopefully be able to identify them because it is only during the pathway to violence that you as a leader or HR manager can intercede and potentially save lives and careers.

It is during this pathway to violence that the company's threat assessment team can engage with their partners in law enforcement, or the medical field, to get help to the person stuck in that pathway cycle.

So, what does the pathway look like?

According to Weston and Calhoun, the cycle consists of the following stages:

- Grievance
- Ideation
- Planning
- Preparation
- Act (of Violence)

The first part of the cycle is the grievance stage. The grievance stage occurs when something bad happens to a person. In our case, it is when something bad happens to an employee that we lead, or to whom we provide HR services.

It can be the employee who gets terminated, gets suspended, or gets counseled for his/her performance in the workplace. Or, it can be the employee that fails to get that raise or promotion he thought he deserved. It could be one of a thousand bad things that befall human beings on a daily basis. To most people, when these bad things happen, they grieve for a short period of time and then move on. But there is a small portion of the population, that moves from the grievance phase to the next phase, which is the ideation phase.

The ideation phase occurs when the grieved person then gets the idea that his grievance, i.e. the termination or suspension, is the fault of someone or something, and that violence is the only reasonable response. So, our disciplined employee might blame his suspension on his immediate supervisor or his cubicle mate. The aggrieved person gets fixated that they can assign blame for their grievance to an individual or organization. The person in this stage does not take personal responsibility for his actions that resulted in the grievance but instead focuses all of his energy and animus towards the person or entity that is the target of his grievance.

The experts in threat assessment found that people who commit targeted violence in the workplace, move from the ideation phase to the planning phase. In the planning phase, the subject decides to take action against the person, place, or thing that caused him to be wronged. So, in this phase, the individual starts to hatch a plan to get even. It is at this time that the potential attacker decides how to institute the violent plan. At this point, the attacker might decide to attack his 'nemesis' at the workplace with a knife or to attack his entire working group by using a firearm. After creating a plan, the potential attacker then moves to the preparation phase. This is the stage where the guns are purchased and test-fired at the range. The clothing that the attacker wants to wear is purchased or laid out. Maybe the attacker drives the route to the site or conducts surveillance of the target of his grievance.

The final stage of the pathway to violence occurs at the attack stage. There is no need to discuss this stage any further. We have seen it too many times before. We saw it at Parkland High School, we saw it at Columbine, and we have seen it in work-places across the country about once every couple of weeks. It is too late for business leaders and HR professionals to act during this final phase. Violence is inevitable at this point. You hope that your employees have taken your run/hide/fight pre-sentations seriously. This is the very reason why you, the reader of this book, needs to know this process so that they can be identified when the pre-attack stages are occurring, and hopefully, do what you can to thwart the upcoming attack.

So, let's look at the Oklahoma City bombing through the eyes of the pathway to violence. I am no expert on that subject, but as a former Secret Service agent, I know that I lost six Secret Service colleagues to that bombing, and I have a general understanding of that act of terror. When examining that act, it can be said that Timothy McVeigh was aggrieved when he saw what happened at the Branch Davidian compound in Waco, Texas, and during the incident at Ruby Ridge, Idaho. He saw the deaths (his grievance) of people at those two loca-tions, and he blamed the U.S government (the ideation) for those deaths. McVeigh made plans in his head, and on paper, about how to get even. He thought about many ways and many locations but, in the end, he decided to use a bomb at a federal building. He made sure it was a federal building that housed agents from ATF. To McVeigh, his building selection was only made better by the presence of daycare on the first floor of the building. McVeigh then moved to the preparation portion, buying and storing the fertilizer, renting the truck, pre-positioning a crappy Mercury Marquis around the corner from the federal building, etc. etc....and then the plan moved to the attack stage, and one hundred and sixty-eight people were killed, and thousands of lives were destroyed.

That is what the pathway to violence looks like in real life. It is important for you as an organizational leader or HR representative to know what the pathway to violence looks like, so you can recognize it in progress before the act of violence occurs.

Threat Assessment Concept #5
Significant Life Stressors

As a secret service agent, I (like every other agent) conducted many protective intelligence (PI) cases during my career. PI cases are threat assessment cases, the only difference is that the threat is against the most powerful leader in the world, or the vice president, or their families, or against one of the other dozens of people whom the US Secret Service protects. In a PI case, the case agent had to identify who the threat was, assess that threat, and then manage that threat. One of the factors that secret service agents want to know about any potential threat, once he/she was positively identified, was the question of significant life stressors. Unless the threat was from a terrorist, life stressors played an important role in the investigation. Why is this the case and what are significant life stressors?

I knew what every other agent knew, and that is the fact that many attackers and mass murderers have experienced at least one significant life stressor either immediately before the attack or at least within the last year of the attack. So, what is a significant life stressor? The FBI says that a stressor can be anything in the subject's life that causes tension or anxiety. The FBI also states that generally, the more stressors that exist in a person's life, the more difficult it will be for him/her to cope with the stress (Federal Bureau of Investigation 2018). In Appendix A of the same report that I just cited above, the FBI lists a whole series of life events that could be categorized as significant life stressors, but in the interest of brevity I will list some for illustrative purposes:

- Death of a friend or loved one
- Divorce
- Financial strain
- Marital problems
- Physical injury/pain

In 2018, the U.S. Secret Service National Threat Assessment Center conducted a study of all mass attacks that took place in 2017. In that study, the USSS looked at twenty-eight incidents of mass attacks in the U.S. that resulted in the deaths of one hundred and forty-seven people and injured seven hundred others. As it relates to significant stressors, the study revealed that all of the attackers had at least one significant stressor in the five years preceding the attacks. The Secret Service singled out the fact that over half of the attackers had experienced a stressor related to financial instability in the five-year period before the attacks (U.S. Secret Service, 2018, p. 5).

So, as the leader of an organization or an HR professional, or even as the member of your organization's threat assessment team, you should be looking for significant life stressors in your subject's past, and also attempt to ascertain if there are any impending significant life stressors in their future, i.e. loss of a job, medical issues, etc.

In a review of school shootings and the people that perpetrated them, the U.S. Secret Service shows the importance of stressors on those that commit targeted violence. The USSS states, "It is widely recognized that high-stress levels are associated with emotional and behavioral problems for children. In their study, the USSS showed that one hundred percent of the attackers experienced stressors, with nearly all of the attackers (94%) experiencing at least one in the six months prior to their attack, and three-quarters of the attackers experiencing a significant stressor within one month of the attack" (U.S. Secret Service 2004).

The studies I have reviewed don't allege that life stressors cause the targeted violence, but it is a factor in almost all targeted violence attacks, especially if the subject is what the FBI calls a "brittle person." I had never used or heard the term "brittle people" until I read the FBI's report "Making Prevention a Reality,"; on page twenty-eight of that report, the authors discuss grievances and that most grieved people don't start on the path to targeted violence. Most people find ways to adapt and overcome. But the FBI states that certain people who are aggrieved are most at risk for committing targeted violence. Those people are termed brittle by the FBI. They are people who:

- Are unable to take rejection.
- Don't handle slights or insults well.
- Claim to be persecuted by others.
- Claim to be isolated and ostracized.
- Perceive themselves as outsiders in their family or organization.
- Can't formulate a healthy response to losses.
- Sulk and obsess over every small perceived injustice to them.
- Often have suicidal ideations.

I have often heard these people being called (and this is what I routinely call them as well) grievance collectors. We have all worked with a grievance collector. They are potentially dangerous in the workplace. Whether you refer to them as brittle or as a grievance collector, you need to be aware of them in your organization. Not all grievance collectors will commit

an act of violence, but many targeted attackers are grievance collectors.

Threat Assessment Concept #6
Concerning Behaviors and Concerning Communications

Human Resource personnel and organizational leaders should
be aware that many attackers engage in "concerning behaviors" and "concerning communications" before they attack.
This is beneficial to leaders because it once again allows us
to identify potential threats in the workplace, and hopefully
intercede before an act of violence is committed. What do I
mean by the concerning behaviors? The FBI writes that "concerning behaviors are *observable* behaviors exhibited by the
attacker...they could be related to potential symptoms of a
mental health disorder, interpersonal interactions, recklessness,
violent media usage, changes in hygiene, and weight, and
physical aggression" (Federal Bureau of Investigation 2018, 17).
In that report, the FBI states that most attackers they studied
had displayed an average of 4.7 concerning behaviors before
the attack. In that study, more than half of the attackers had
displayed concerning behaviors involving mental health issues,
interpersonal interactions, leakage warning behaviors, and
the quality of the person's thinking and communication skills.
Almost half of the attackers had shown concerning behaviors
in work performance or school performance prior to the attack.
This same report documented that majority of attackers had

displayed the first instance of concerning behavior over twenty-five months before the attack.

In the Secret Service report on school shooters, the agency listed the ten most common concerning behaviors exhibited by attackers prior to their attack. Listed below are those concerning behaviors:

1. Threats to the target
2. Intense or escalating anger
3. Interest in weapons
4. Sadness, depression, or isolation
5. Changes in behavior or appearance
6. Suicidal ideations or self-harm
7. Interest in violence
8. Talking about being bullied
9. Poor grades/performance
10. Harassing others

    - (U.S. Secret Service 2019, 45-46)

As organizational leaders, we need to be aware when our employees start exhibiting these behaviors. These types of behaviors don't predict workplace violence particularly but taken in concert with other behaviors, it may alert you that further action should be taken. One of the behaviors that potential attackers might engage in is "concerning communications." The Secret Service relates that a person's communications (especially threats) can provide an insight into a subject's intent, their mindset, and their motivations. In a Secret Service study, they report that eighty-nine percent of attackers had engaged in "in-person concerning communications" before they attacked. The same report details that a majority of attackers had relayed a concerning electronic message before the attack. About half of the attackers had placed a concerning online post, at some time, before the attack (U.S. Secret Service 2019, 46).

The FBI divides "concerning communications" into two distinct categories, either as:

(1) direct threats and/or confrontations, or

(2) leakage, which is revealing clues that might show the intent to attack.

In a recent study, the FBI shows "that more than half of the attackers they studied had made threats or had a prior confrontation before that attack" (Federal Bureau of Investigation 2018, 24).

Regarding leakage, the FBI found that it is more prevalent in adolescents, but that even in the adults they studied, over half of the attackers had leaked their intent to commit violence.

Having read the last few sentences, you might get a false sense of security that threats always precede an act of violence.

That is not the case. In fact, the FBI stated that "although more than half of the active shooters with pre-attack targets made threats, in the majority of the overall cases no threats were made to a target, and the FBI cautions that the absence of a direct threat should not be falsely reassuring to those assessing the potential for violence raised by other circumstances and factors" (Federal Bureau of Investigation 2018,. 25).

Threat Assessment Concept #7
Hunters versus Howlers

Following up on the last section, not all threat makers commit violence and many attackers don't make threats. The phrase "Hunters and Howlers" comes from the work of author Frederick S. Calhoun, in his book of the same name. In that book, Calhoun details the history of the US Marshals, especially as it relates to the Marshals' responsibility to provide protection to federal judges and to investigate people who make or pose threats to those judges. The book details the storied history of the US Marshals Service and discusses specific cases where people either assaulted federal judges or made threats against them. As the author makes very clear, most of the people who made threats against the federal judiciary never attempted to carry them out. Calhoun also points out that those people who did attack federal judges never made a threat before-hand. In short, the author states that hunters hunt and howlers howl. As a business leader or HR professional, you need to be aware that many times it is not the person who makes a threat that you need to worry about, but is, in fact, the person that is in the periphery, sulking and planning, and is knee-deep in the pathway to violence, that you need to concern yourself with.

I can tell you that the Secret Service has found out that more often than not, the person who threatens a Secret Service protectee often poses little danger to them. The people who have been the greatest danger to our nation's leaders have always been those people who have hatched their plan in silence and never gave advance notice of their motives. As a manager, business leader, or HR representative, you should be aware that hunters hunt and howlers howl. You may find yourself very worried about the howlers, and you should not ignore them. But, in your position, it is the hunters that pose the biggest threat to you, your company, and your employees.

Threat Assessment Concept #8
Narcissism and Psychopathy

As I mentioned early on, I am a member of ATAP, the Association of Threat Assessment Professionals. When I was studying for the certified threat manager exam for ATAP, all test takers were asked to read a book by Paul Babiak and Robert D. Hare entitled *Snakes in Suits: When Psychopaths go to Work.*

I have known a few psychopaths in my day and I have even worked with a few. Actually, I might have dated one just before meeting my wife. I think we have all been exposed to a psychopath or two. As for the book, I highly recommend it for business leaders and HR types.

Babiak and Hare write that psychopaths:

- Commit more crimes, more violent crimes, and a greater variety of crimes than other criminals.
- Are more controlling, aggressive, threatening, and abusive than other criminals.
- Commit predatory violence as opposed to reactive violence.
- Makeup fifteen percent of the prison population, even though one percent of the general population are psychopaths.
- Psychopaths are responsible for at least half of the serious crimes in North America.
- Possess no conscience, are incapable of feeling empathy, and are only loyal to themselves.

Of immediate concern for the leader of any group is the threat that psychopaths can be to the organization and its members. Babiak and Hare state that psychopaths:

- Are difficult to be seen for who they are.
- Have a talent for reading people and sizing them up.
- Possess excellent verbal skills.
- Are social chameleons.

- Are motivated to take advantage of people.

- Are master manipulators.

The book's authors state that psychopaths use a five-step process to gain access to the corporation and then gain and maintain power. The five steps are:

1. Entry

2. Assessment

3. Manipulation

4. Confrontation

5. Ascension

The authors write that psychopaths at work see everyone as one of three types of people. They see their co-workers as either pawn, patrons, or as patsies. In their book, Babiak and Hare provide guidance on thoroughly screening for psychopaths in the application stage, and they discuss the red flags to look for during the hiring process. We can't do justice to a three hundred and thirty-six page book here, but suffice it to say that anyone who leads or serves people in an organization should read this book.

The Secret Service also documents why narcissism is problematic in the workplace. In their report regarding mass attacks in the U.S., the Secret Service wrote that eighty-two percent of the mass attackers in 2017 had "exhibited behaviors consistent with aggressive narcissism, as evidenced by displays of rigidness, hostility, or extreme self-centeredness. For example, some of the attackers had inappropriately asserted control over others, as observed by their histories of domestic violence, sexual assault, harassment or harming of animals. Others had a history of violent or angry outbursts following interpersonal conflicts with co-workers, neighbors, or family members. Some attackers displayed an inflated sense of self or entitlement, unrealistically believing that they were deserving of certain relationships, successes, or benefits, with some reacting angrily when they did not obtain what they believed they deserved" (U.S. Secret Service 2018, 5).

As leaders of your organization, you should be ensuring that your applicant screening process is looking to eliminate psychopaths and narcissists from your organization. Once aboard your organization, they pose a threat in more ways than one.

Threat Assessment Concept #9
Threat Enhancers versus Mitigators/inhibitors

The field of threat assessment has identified certain factors that tend to keep people from the pathway of violence. Those factors, called inhibitors or mitigators, do what their name portrays, they tend to inhibit or mitigate violent action by a person. The reverse is also true, there are certain factors, called threat enhancers, that tend to be associated with increasing the likelihood of violence. We could write an entire book on this very subject and there are numerous books we could recommend, but for the sake of this book where we introduce concepts, we will provide a list of enhancers and mitigators. I took the list of the below enhancers and mitigators from an FBI study. The study is available online and provides a comprehensive look at identifying, assessing, and managing potential threats (U.S. Department of Justice 2017).

Let's start with the good news first. The field of threat assessment tells us that if you are dealing with a potential threat in the workplace, look for certain factors that, when present, may prevent the potential threat from completing an act of targeted violence. The following is not a comprehensive list, but is a good starting point to show you the types of factors that can prevent action by certain subjects:

- Does the subject have, and has he/she ever, maintained a sense of humor?
- Does the subject have positive influences around him/her (supportive family or significant other)?
- Does the subject have access to social supports (friends, counselors, church, clubs)?
- Does the subject have positive outlets for his stress (hobbies, sports, exercise)?
- Does the subject maintain a set of positive and realistic goals?

So, now for the bad news. There are certain factors that tend to be associated with increased risk of violence:

- Has the subject ever stalked or threatened someone in the past?

- Does the subject have "boundary issues?"

- Is there an absence of a support system or family for the subject?

- Is the subject physically or emotionally isolated?

- Does the subject have a history of violence?

- Speaking of violence, does the subject have a history of being exposed to violence when young?

- Does the subject have a substance abuse problem?

- Does the subject have a history of suicidal ideation?

- Does the subject suffer from a personality disorder or mental illness?

- Does the subject have easy access to firearms or explosives?

As leaders, we should attempt to keep our employees from feeling isolated. We should look to encourage mitigators in their lives, especially their work lives. We should be aware of employees with one or more of the enhancers.

Threat Assessment Concept #10
Pre-Attack Behaviors of Active Shooters

The FBI released a report that is considered to be the 'Holy Grail,' as it relates to what activities active shooters undertake before engaging in their deadly plan. The report is called "A

Study of Pre-Attack Behaviors of Active Shooters in the United States between 2000 and 2013." This report, covering active shooter incidents in the United States over a thirteen-year period, examines specific behaviors that may precede an attack and that might be useful in identifying, assessing, and managing those who may be on a pathway to violence. The report can be found at the following link: www.fbi.gov/file-repository/pre-attack-behaviors-of-active-shooters-in-us-2000-2013.pdf/view

Below, I have included some of the facts from the report that I think organizational leaders and HR professionals need to know.

The following comes directly from the FBI report (Federal Bureau of Investigation, 2018):

- Active shooters do not snap, they take time to plan and prepare for the attack, with the vast majority spending a week or longer planning their attack.

- Only twenty-five percent of the active shooters had ever been diagnosed with a mental illness.

- Active shooters typically experienced multiple stressors in the year before they attacked.

- The age of the shooters in the study ranged from twelve years to eighty-eight years old.

- The shooters were overwhelmingly male (94%) and white (63%).

- The shooters were mostly single.

- Each active shooter displayed on average four to five concerning behavior to others.

- Many of the shooters, whose grievances could be identified, were associated with an adverse interpersonal or employment action.

- In the majority of the cases, at least one of the shooter's victims was specifically targeted by the shooter.

- Firearms (legally obtained) were the weapon of choice.

- About half of the shooters had suicidal ideations or had engaged in suicide-related behavior at some point in time before the attack.

- A vast majority of the shooters did not make a direct threat against their target.

If you hold a leadership role within your organization, I would respectfully request that you take a few minutes and read this report. It won't take long, but I truly believe it will give you a different perspective the next time you are making decisions about terminations, counseling, or addressing the odd behavior recently displayed by Fred in Accounting.

Threat Assessment Concept #11
Threat Assessment Teams in Corporate America

If you are reading this book, it is reasonable to believe that you are a business leader or an HR type and that you are employed in the private sector. If your company is large enough, say at least a couple of hundred employees, I pray that your company or organization maintains a threat assessment team (TAT). Different companies may call these teams by different names, or by different acronyms, but in short, the team's goal is to identify potential problems, assess the risk posed by those problems, and most importantly, are tasked with finding possible solutions to mitigate the threats posed to employees and the organization.

The TAT, more than likely, is relatively small in nature, maybe five to ten people, and should be multi-disciplinary. Most TAT's incorporate representatives from Human Resources, the Security department, Legal Counsel, the Safety department, and/or any other department that might be of relevance. Sometimes corporate threat assessment teams will invite outside entities like local law enforcement or mental health practitioners. TAT members must be selected for both their technical skills and institutional knowledge, but it is as important that they are selected because of their professionalism, their ability to be trusted with sensitive and personal information. The average TAT member needs to be a team player and must be innovative and a problem solver. The TAT members should have attended a formal training course, usually taught by outside vendors, that discusses workplace violence, threat assessment, mental health issues, and applicable criminal statutes in their location. TAT members are usually volunteers who take on the TAT role as an ancillary responsibility to their usual jobs. The TAT can meet at routine intervals to discuss policies and procedures but are intended to meet when information is received of a problematic employee, or any other incident is brought to their attention. If your organization does not have a TAT, you should consider instituting one. I would recommend reading Chapter five of the FBI's report entitled "Making Prevention a Reality." It can be accessed online at www.fbi.gov/file-repository/making-prevention-a-reality.pdf/view

It walks the reader through the entire process of what a threat assessment team is and how to go about instituting one. (U.S. Department of Justice 2017)

As you read this, you probably see the need for threat assessment teams in your organization but to what end? You are probably asking how a TAT solves the problem? Well, once a TAT identifies the threat and makes an assessment of the threat, then it is incumbent on them to manage the threat. The TAT can intervene in the process and seek out certain strategies to prevent or stop impending potential violent action. Some of their options include but are not limited to:

1. Seeking the arrest of the subject.
2. Requesting hospitalization of the subject.
3. Seeking a restraining order or protective order.
4. Referring to the subject to outpatient counseling.
5. Asking the subject's social network (family/friends) to assist the subject and influence positive behavior.

6. Seeking corporate administrative actions (termination, suspension, etc.).

As a leader, you should know that threat assessment teams are the best business practice for identifying and proactively addressing the problem of workplace violence.

Threat Assessment Concept #12
The Rise of Red Flag Laws and Risk Protection Orders

One of the options that a threat assessment team might use (depending on the state of occurrence) is to request the use of the state's red flag law. Red flag laws, sometimes called 'Extreme Risk Protection Orders (ERPO's),' allow courts to issue orders to temporarily confiscate the firearms of individuals deemed to be a risk to others or themselves. Depending on the state you reside in, ERPO laws allow family members and/or law enforcement to go to court and appear before a judge to request an order that would confiscate the guns of an individual who they believe poses a threat to themselves or anyone else. ERPO petitioners must present evidence to the court on why the individual poses a threat to others, as well as to himself/herself.

- As I write this, about fifteen states have instituted some type of red flag law, some with success and some not. Currently, there is turmoil in Virginia about a state law that would allow gun confiscation. To be honest, I don't know where I stand on this issue of red flag laws.

- As a former law enforcer and current threat assessor, I absolutely would welcome the ability to remove readily accessible weapons from the possession of a viable threat. After all, we know that firearms, especially legally owned firearms, is the attacker's usual weapon of choice.

- As a gun owner and a believer in the right to keep and bear arms, I worry about diminishing the rights that our founding fathers listed in the Bill of Rights.

- As a former cop, I worry about the safety of the police officers attempting to confiscate guns from people that have not actually committed a crime yet.

- As a pragmatist and a realist, I know that taking guns from someone's home, doesn't make the situation entirely safe. The potentially violent person can buy, borrow, or steal another gun, or simply use some other type of weapon, like a knife or even their automobile to perpetrate violence.

- As a threat assessor, I know that threat assessment is an art and a science. I know that threat assessors can make mistakes, and I know that threat assessors cannot predict future behavior. We don't live in Tom Cruise's *Minority Report* where cops work in the "Pre-crime" division and are able to predict future criminal acts.

- As a layman, I wonder if the act of forcibly taking property away from someone that has not yet been formally charged with a crime might just be the straw that breaks the back of a brittle person, causing them to actually commit the violent act we worry they might potentially commit.

So, if I don't even have a fully formed opinion on the subject (and I do this stuff for a living) why bring it up in this book? You as an organizational leader or HR professional need to know what tools you have available to you. If all of a sudden Fred in Accounting has conducted himself in a way that leads you to believe he is a danger to you or your employees, you need to know your options. You should know whether your state has a red flag law, what it says, and who can go about petitioning for one.

Threat Assessment Concept #13
Miscellaneous and Random Thoughts and Observations on Threat Assessment Issues

Prevention not Prediction: All threat assessors will tell you that they are not soothsayers, they cannot foretell the future. As the FBI says in "Making Prevention a Reality"- *The perfect threat management solution cannot be foreseen. The threat assessment and threat management relationship is one of continuous reassessment and modification. Without the benefit of hindsight, however, threat managers cannot know at what point an intervention would have been effective. Prevention, therefore, is best approached in a holistic way. Thinking about the person of concern, the target, the situation and the setting in their totality increases the odds of preventing a tragedy.*

- (U.S. Department of Justice 2017, 53)

The Relationship between Homicide and Suicide: As a cop, I was often told that there is a thin line between suicide and homicide. Many veteran cops, especially my field training officers would warn me that when dealing with suicidal persons, be very aware that if the person is intent on killing themselves, it doesn't take much to move them to also kill a cop or family member attempting to intercede. In "Making Prevention a Reality," the FBI writes- *Homicide and suicide are more closely linked than many think. In many cases, multiple homicides are linked with prior suicide attempts, gestures, or suicidal ideation on the part of the perpetrator. This is especially true with targeted violence. A research project revealed that 78% of targeted mass attackers exhibited a history of suicide attempts or suicidal thoughts at some point prior to the attack. Moreover, many offenders attempt or succeed at suicide or suicide by cop at the conclusion of a targeted violence event.*

- (U.S. Department of Justice 2017, 26)

The L.A. Times Research: Although I am not always a fan of mainstream media, I highly suggest to the readers of this book that they take a look at the writing of the L.A. Times, as it relates to their research on mass killers. The L.A. Times participated in a project funded by the U.S. Department of Justice where they studied one hundred and seventy-one mass shootings in public spaces during the time period of 1966 through 2019. Their criteria were that there had to be four or more people killed in the event. The LA Times review showed that ninety-eight percent of mass shooters were men, that fifty-two percent of the shooters were white, and that seventy percent of the killers knew at least some of their victims. As a result of their research, The LA Times states that there are actually five types of mass shooters which include the following:

1. K-12 school shooters

2. College and university school shooters

3. Workplace shooters

4. House of worship shooters

5. Retail/restaurant shooters.

With regards to the workplace shooter, The LA Times states that the shooter is usually a male (96%) in his 40s. The LA Times states that workplace shooters don't have racial consistency (40% white, 30% black, and 10% Latino). Possibly significant for our readers, the LA Times states that "alterations to building design and conducting active shooter drills are likely to be ineffective since the shooter is usually an insider, well-rehearsed in the security procedures" (Densley 2019). I encourage you to read the LA Times research. It is interesting to gain their perspective on the subject matter.

CHAPTER SEVEN

"FREE ADVICE"

Your authors have spent decades in public safety and corporate security. We wish for nothing else than safe and trouble-free work environments for you and your employees. The following musings did not fit into any of the other sections of the book, but we wanted to pass these tidbits on to you for whatever it is worth.

- If you are an organizational leader or HR professional, please take some time to develop a relationship with your state, local, and federal law enforcement agencies and personnel. Get to know the patrol officer (on all three shifts) who patrol the area where your facility is located. If possible, get to know the detective in your location that handles workplace violence investigations, or the agency's threat assessment specialist. The time to do that is before you need their help, not during an incident or after an incident. Having a pre-formed relationship with these officers will pay huge dividends for both parties. This relationship-building will take some effort but it will pay off in the long run.

So, how do you go about this process? How about flagging down the patrol officer you see driving through your parking lot, identifying yourself, and taking ten minutes to walk him/her through your facility? Exchange business cards, allow the officer access to the company's snack bar or dining area. Maybe allow the officer(s) access to the company's gym? Maybe allow them access to your restrooms or cafeteria after hours so that they can write reports in a safe environment? As a former cop, I can tell you that when you are on the midnight shift, a safe, warm, and private restroom is a rare commodity. Little things like that will make you be seen as a partner to the agency.

Don't misunderstand me here, I am not saying give them preferential treatment because you expect something in return. Cops will respond to you and provide professional service to you in every circumstance. It doesn't matter if you are a stranger to them or if you are known to them. But, you know this fact, interpersonal relationships, and networking are key to every successful venture. It is no different when creating a workplace free from violence.

Consider this, Fred in Accounting starts acting weird and your company's threat assessment team is worried. Is that the time to try and find the most appropriate police contact to assist you, or would you rather call someone you have a relationship with, explain the situation, and seek their counsel on the next steps?

I currently live in Maine. My house is heated with fuel oil. I established a relationship with my fuel oil company. In fact, I pay $100 a year to be part of their protection plan. In essence, I have a trusted network now, and I created a relationship in order to achieve greater results. What does that protection plan get me? If my home heating service ever breaks down, they will respond 24-7 and fix my equipment with no service fee. If I need the delivery of fuel, I go to the top of the list because I have an established relationship. The same goes for your organization. When it hits the fan, is that the appropriate time to build a relationship with your public safety partners?

Consider attending a citizen's police academy sponsored by your local police department. Make contacts that way. Consider joining the FBI's InfraGard program as a corporate member, or seek out your local Secret Service office and see if you can participate in that agency's electronic crimes task force as a corporate partner. Consider inviting your local police chief to speak to an all-hands meeting on some subject. What about hosting a public safety open house at your facility? Another great tool is offering up your facility to the local SWAT team (after hours, of course) and allowing them to train for an active shooter scenario in a real-world business environment. In my last role as a corporate security director, our facility had a huge unused parking lot. With the signatures on a few waiver forms, I was able to offer to the police department and Sheriff's office, the use of those parking lots for high-speed pursuit training and other types of vehicle training. It literally cost me and the company nothing, but we created goodwill and relationships between my company and the local first responders.

- As an organizational leader or HR professional, I would ask you to develop a close working relationship with your security professional, and that if you are making any type of personnel decision, to please ask yourself this question: Could this decision have any impact on the safety and security of employees or this facility? If the answer is yes, then please consult with your security professional. The reason we ask you to do this is because security folks and HR folks, or security and upper management, often have completely different mindsets and worldviews. Often one group doesn't understand the other, and if they don't seek input from each other on important matters, there might be dire consequences. Let me give you a case that I am somewhat familiar with and highlight the two worldviews. Let's say there was a manager in Accounting, you guessed it, and his name is Fred. Fred supervises four other employees, all attractive young females. Fred has an engaging management style and loves to joke around with his subordinates. Fred is a huge martial artist and there are some rumors in the workplace that Fred acquired his recent athletic body through the use of some pharmaceuticals, namely steroids. Fred is an extremely gifted accountant and is an institution at the facility.

One day, one of Fred's subordinate employees approaches HR and suggests that Fred is engaging in sexually harassing behaviors. HR does not confide with security about this issue. Fred is counseled by HR and it doesn't go well. HR doesn't tell security that Fred became "problematic" in the counseling session. HR feels that Fred is in denial. One of Fred's employees (one of the ones that didn't make the harassment claim) submits her resignation letter and leaves the next day. The only thing HR advises security to do, at that point, was to remove badge access for the resigning employee. Within a week, the employee that brought the allegations submits her resignation letter. HR never advises security about anything other than to disable the second employee's badge. This is a failure in the system. HR and security need to work together. Now, having said that, security must know that they always have to maintain the confidentiality and privacy rights in these types of matters. But HR never once briefed security on this matter. Hopefully, if you are reading this paragraph, you see that Fred is potentially a threat to the workplace and the Security Director should have been brought into the mix.

- I would suggest that if you are reading this book, you realize that threats and threat assessment are two issues you need to deal with in your profession. I would ask you to consider joining the Association of Threat Assessment Professionals (ATAP). I have belonged to many professional groups during my career but none as impressive as ATAP. I have attended many of the training sessions and their twice-yearly conferences. I come away from those offerings smarter, and better prepared to deal with conflict and violence in the workplace. Speaking of their seminars, they have a relationship with the Disney corporation, and they offer winter training at Disney World every January, and a Disney Land conference every summer.

- We highly recommend that every organizational leader or HR professional obtain, read, and keep as a reference, the book that is a joint project between the Society of Human Resource Management (SHRM) and the American Society of Industrial Security (ASIS). The book is entitled *Workplace Violence Prevention and Intervention Standard 2011*. It is a relatively short book, less than sixty pages, but is highly informative and comprehensive. It provides a great background on the subject and walks any office professional through the subject matter.

- You are hopefully providing some type of professional active shooter training to your personnel. In a perfect world, you would provide this at new hire orientation and again at least annually. Nothing scary or crazy, but sound advice and situational awareness. If you are discussing the run, hide, fight protocols or any of the other types of training out there, your folks will be looking for locations in your facilities that could be used if they had to shelter in place (the "hide" portion of run, hide, fight). These locations should be easily fortified (able to lock the door or block the door), should have few windows, and preferably walls made of something other than glass or drywall. In my role as security director, I found a product that I recommend to help harden many of these rooms. I receive no remuneration from this company but I was highly impressed by their product. In all transparency, I did develop a friendship with the management team of the company, so please accept the lie of the green. But again, I receive no compensation for recommending their products. The company is called Campus Safety Products and the product that I recommend is their 'Rhinoware Door Barricade system." The company's website and description of their products can be found at https://campussafetyprod-ucts.com/rhinoware.php

CHAPTER EIGHT

"CONCLUSION"

We hope that in the preceding chapters we have made a successful case that business leaders and HR professionals can benefit from what cops and threat assessors already know. Our goal, when we started the book, was to add tools to your toolbox. Our intent was to never scare you or alarm you but to prepare you and provide you with the blueprint for a new mindset. What we hoped to do was to better prepare you for when your organization experiences that bump in the night. Ideally, we wanted to prevent those bumps. Doing nothing while you wait for the other shoe to drop is not the way that leaders deal with potential, foreseeable problems.

We began the book by stating that everyone has a purpose, but not everyone was meant to be a cop, a threat assessment specialist, or even a milkman. We appreciate what you do as an organizational leader or as a member of the Human

Resources field. We said we would offer our concepts to you in a buffet style. We hope you took what you wanted and left the rest. We pray that we gave you enough to chew on, and left you with some decisions to make and some mindsets to change.

Your two authors are available via email to hopefully answer any questions you might still have. You can reach us at- trustandconfidencekr@gmail.com

We would love your feedback or questions.

We would welcome the opportunity to speak to your group or to provide you, or your team, with training that is realistic, informative, and fun. If interested, please take a second and check out our website at www.trustandconfidence.org

We wish you long, safe and healthy careers.

Kevin and Phil.

WORKS CITED

Hare, Robert D, and Paul Babiak. *Snakes in Suit: When Psychopaths Go to Work*. New York City: Harper Collins, 2006.

"Improving Survival from Active Shooter Events: The Hartford Consensus." The Bulletin, July 29, 2014. https://bulletin.facs. org/2013/06/improving-survival-from-active-shooter-ev.

Densley, J.P. "Opinion: There Is No Single Profile of a Mass Shooter. Our Data Show There Are Five Types." *The LA Times*, November 14, 2019. www.latimes.com/opinion/story/2019-11-14/ the-five-types-of-mass-shooters.

Ellifritz, Greg. "How to Spot a Bad Guy- A Comprehensive Look at Body Language and Pre-Assault Indicators." Active Response Training, April 27, 2020. https://www.activeresponsetraining. net/how-to-spot-a-bad-guy-a-comprehensive-look-at-body-language-and-pre-assault-indicators.

"History of ICS." EMSI. Accessed March 25, 2020. http://www. emsics.com/history-of-ics/.

"A Study of the Pre-Attack Behaviors of Active Shooters in the United States between 2000-2013." FBI. U.S Department of Justice, Washington DC., 2018.

Holtz, Lou. *Winning Every Day: The Game Plan for Success*. New York City: Harper Collins, 1998.

"Making Prevention a Reality: Identifying, Assessing, and Managing the Threat of Targeted Attacks." FBI. FBI, February 24, 2017. https://www.fbi.gov/file-repository/making-prevention-a-reality.pdf/view.

Lebron, A. . *The Latest on Workplace Violence*. (2019, 04 19). Retrieved from Rave Mobile Safety: www.ravemobilesafety.com

Pane, Lisa Marie. "US Mass Killings Hit New High in 2019, Most Were Shootings." AP NEWS. Associated Press, December 23, 2019. https://apnews.com/4441ae68d14e61b64110db44f906af92.

Richards, Ron. Command presence, May 2004. http://www.withthecommand.com/2004-May/PA-Richards-commandpresence.html.

Scalora, Mario J. "Home." Targeted Violence Research Team | Nebraska. Accessed 5AD. https://psychology.unl.edu/targeted-violence/home.

Sherwood, Ben. *The Survivors Club: The Secrets and Science That Could Save Your Life*. New York City: Grand Central Publishing, 2009.

Threat Assessment in Schools: A Guide to Managing Threatening Situations and Creating Safe School Climates. Washington DC: U.S Secret Service, 2004.

Mass Attacks in Public Spaces-2017. Washington DC: U.S Secret Services, 2018.

Protecting America's Schools: A U.S. Secret Service Analysis of Targeted School Violence. Washington DC: U.S Secret Service, 2019.

Calhoun, Frederik S, and Stephen W Weston. *Contemporary Threat Management: A Practical Guide for Identifying, Assessing, and Managing Individuals of Violent Intent.* San Diego: Specialized Training Services, 2003.